T0051767

THE
JOY OF
BEING
SELFISH

THE
JOY OF
BEING
SELFISH

Why you need <u>boundaries</u> and how to set them!

MICHELLE ELMAN

WELBECK

Published by Welbeck
An imprint of Welbeck Non-Fiction Limited,
part of Welbeck Publishing Group.
20 Mortimer Street,
London W1T 3JW

First published by Welbeck in 2021

Copyright © Michelle Elman, 2021

Michelle Elman has asserted her right under the Copyright, Designs and
Patents Act, 1988, to be identified as Author of this work.

All rights reserved. No part of this publication may be reproduced, stored
in a retrieval system, or transmitted in any form or by any means,
electronically, mechanical, photocopying, recording or otherwise, without
the prior permission of the copyright owners and the publishers.

A CIP catalogue record for this book is available from the British Library

ISBN
Hardback – 9781802790252

Typeset by IDSUK (DataConnection) Ltd.
Printed at CPI UK
2 4 6 8 10 9 7 5 3 1

www.welbeckpublishing.com

For every woman who has been treated badly and wondered whether you deserved it – you don't.

AUTHOR'S NOTE

Some of the names and identifying details in this book have been changed to protect the privacy of the people in the examples used. All stories involving clients have been included with their permission.

CONTENTS

CHAPTER 1
INTRODUCTION

Selfish (adj.): Seeking or concentrating on one's own advantage, pleasure or well-being without regard for others

Self-love is a concept everyone can get on board with – as long as you have done what you need to do for everyone else first. The problem is, once you've done that, there is usually no time or energy left for yourself. Often, we are so quick to take care of others, but it is important to recognize that there is a cost to this: you. It's coming at the expense of your own self-care. Here is where boundaries become important. Boundaries are the practical side of self-love. It's the part that no one wants to talk about because it flies in the face of the narrative that in order to be a good person, you need to put others' needs before your own, and if you do put your needs first and foremost, you are considered selfish. Self-love means saying, "I'm going to love myself and not make it anyone else's job." Setting boundaries means saying, "I'm going to get my needs met and I'm not going to expect others to do it for me." If that's selfish, then I'm selfish.

Controversial or not, I believe in order to have self-love, it is necessary to be selfish. It requires you to reorder your priorities to ensure you come at the top of that list. The word "selfish" holds a stigma in modern society because it is associated with the idea that you have a disregard for other humans. But when you regard others more highly than yourself, the unfortunate consequence is often that you are completely forgotten. I think one of the most loving things you can do for the people around you is to take care of yourself. When you don't, the people in your life often feel a responsibility to do that duty for you.

Conversely, selfless people in our society are often praised – but those who act like they are selfless are hiding behind the fact that they are too scared to ask for what they want. Take the example of the person who is so "selfless" that when you ask them where they want to eat, they don't know. It's your choice and they don't mind, no matter how many times you ask them. It might seem kind of them, but when you are put in this position often enough, it becomes exhausting because you end up having to read their mind. Do they truly not care, or are they just not vocalizing what they truly feel? Many of these people don't know what they want because they either have never been asked, or were so often ignored when they did ask that they stopped asking. Either way, "selflessness" is not about being "good", it's about being liked. It is deriving self-esteem from your usefulness to – and approval by – others, and holding that above your own needs.

The ironic thing is that most people who pride themselves on "selflessness" are not being selfless for others, but actually for themselves. They do everything for others to fill a void in themselves that they are unwilling to confront. They make sacrifices that no one asked them to make, which results in pent-up resentment because no one is taking care of them and their needs. The problem with the "selfless" person is two-fold. There is an assumed uselessness in the party they are helping because when you do things for a person that they should be doing for themselves, inherent in that is the belief that they are not capable enough to manage without you. Then, because that "selfless" person is so involved in your life, they are unable to boundary their opinion because they feel like they have a right to have an opinion on areas in your life that are none of their business. "Mind your own business" is a phrase that is used a lot in these situations but if the selfless person focused more on their own business, they would realize their selflessness is a result of insecurity, and it creates more problems than it fixes. In fact, I believe if we all were "minding our own business" more and being more selfish, there would be fewer judgements and unsolicited opinions; you'd spend time focusing on the resolution of your own problems rather than projecting onto the people around you.

For women in particular, the first step is to believe that you deserve the right to set boundaries in the first place. Women are taught to be martyrs: to empty ourselves out in the service of others, forgetting about our own dreams, ambitions and desires and instead using our time and energy to fuel the people around us. How many gifts has the world been deprived of because that woman does not have the time or energy to fulfil her own dreams? How many important ideas were shelved because pursuing those dreams would have been "selfish"? Societally, women are taught to give, give, give – but when is it our turn to take? What if we flipped it around? Instead of giving so much to others, we could give to ourselves so that we don't need to take so much. We can demonize the people who take, or we can own our stuff and recognize that the problem is not that they take, but that we are unable to say no.

Since this message of needing to be "selfless" and look after others is drilled into women from such a young age, the majority of women get their self-esteem directly from how much they can give to others and be available to everyone's requests. Their value is derived from their usefulness to others and their worth is based on being seen as a good person. Your behaviour cannot define your goodness, because if it does, you are giving others the power to determine what is "good enough". When you stop striving to be seen as a good wife, friend, employee, mother or daughter, it gives you permission to realize that you are a good person not because of what you can give or provide, but because of who you are. Part of boundary setting is realizing your worth is intrinsic. We need to let go of the societal messages we have received about what we need to do to be good to others, and instead start redefining how we need to be good to ourselves.

Learning how to set boundaries might be hard, but living without boundaries is harder – and I would know. I used to be the perfect example of someone living without boundaries. At 18, I had no clue where I ended and someone else began. If you had asked me then what I wanted, I couldn't have told you, and if you asked me to communicate how I actually felt in a situation, I would have been terrified. I was surrounded by co-dependent relationships; my friends would joke that I would answer the phone after one ring. Being a "good friend" was my number-one priority, almost always to the detriment of myself. While that sounds admirable, it was not healthy. My best friend and I, at the time, were so co-dependent that if I turned up to the university bar without her, people would ask me where she was. If a friend wanted to go out and no one would go with them, they always knew I was the one to go to because if they nagged me enough, I would cave. Even if I didn't want to go. Even if I had a deadline the next day. Long story short, I was a pushover.

In terms of my romantic relationships, I would bend over backwards for the person I was dating, and the worst part was that they knew it. One evening, I took an hour to reply to one of my boyfriend's texts and he joked that it was unusual because I was "usually at his beck and call". When I would ask my friends why all my romantic relationships went so wrong, I would hear the same thing: "You are too nice." In hindsight, "too nice" was code for "You have no boundaries." I would rather be liked than say how I actually felt. I would stay silent if someone upset me, and explain away shitty behaviour as "not a big deal". I would release the resentment from those boundary violations with passive-aggressive comments, and worst of all, I would keep people in my life who had no respect for me. I was so shocked any-one would want to spend time with me that I didn't think I had a right or a choice to end a relationship or friendship.

It would take me many more years of learning the hard way to finally be ready to face the fact that my lack of boundaries was not only causing unnecessary drama in my life, but also stress, anxiety, guilt and resentment. In short, boundaries revolutionized my life. It is the single great-est tool I have learnt in all my coaching, and has person-ally changed my life in a way that renders my previous life unrecognizable.

My introduction to boundaries, and everything I have learnt since, came in the form of a person called Michelle Zelli. She was, and still is, my life coach, and is completely responsible for the very boundaried person now writing this book. We met back in 2015 after I became convinced I needed "business coaching". I was a year into being a life coach, and was unsure which direction to go with my busi-ness, and whether I should specialize in a certain area. In our first session, she informed me that I did not need business coaching, I needed life coaching. Throughout our first year working together, I left each session aware of more prob-lems in my life than I thought I had. It was an eye-opening experience. Not only was Michelle showing me all the blind spots in my life, but she was the first woman I had met that so fiercely knew what she wanted and was unafraid to say it. I didn't know how to get that, but I knew I wanted it. Six months into working together, it felt like I had received an endless fountain of information that I couldn't absorb quick enough. I entered 2016 with a greater awareness of my needs and redefined "selfish" as a positive thing. For the first time in my life, I prioritized myself. I finally took notice of the people who put me down or insulted me, and most importantly, I learnt about the power of boundaries. 2017 was going to be the year I put it into action.

Enter my "Year of No". For the whole of 2017, I decided that I was going to live my life according to one simple rule: I was going to say no to anything I didn't want to do and I wasn't going to justify it. At the time, I was in my early twenties and was at a stage where my friendship groups had started fragmenting. Gone were the days of house parties and catching up with everyone in one night. Instead, one-on-one post-work dinners were squeezed into my schedule on the rare evenings I was not working late. I found myself on a never-ending hamster wheel where I never had time for myself. Now that my co-dependency had been dramatically reduced, I started noticing that for the first time in my life, I craved alone time. Without the group dynamic and the convenience of being across the corridor from each other, it started occurring to me that we didn't actually have much in common anymore. I realized that in order to have any alone time at all, I needed to learn how to say no.

INTRODUCTION

The first instance of me saying "no" came late on the evening of 6 January 2017. Somehow I had escaped the first six days of the year without encountering anything that I didn't want to do. A friend called just as I was finishing up work. It had been a long day of tiny frustrating things building up, and he was calling to see if I wanted to go to a pub quiz halfway across London that started in two hours. Without even thinking I said, "Yes, send me the address" and hung up. Crap. The moment I hung up, I knew I had flubbed my resolution already. Yes, I love a pub quiz. Yes, it was a Friday night – but I'm old and 9 p.m. is late and Shoreditch is far. I was *really* looking forward to turning my phone off, watching *Grey's Anatomy* alone and getting an early night. So I called him back.

"I'm not coming anymore."

"Why?" he asked, as I recalled the second part of my resolution to not justify why.

"Just because . . ."

"Because why?"

"Because I said so."

"OK, you are acting weird."

"OK. Have a nice evening! Bye!"

Can you imagine if one of your closest friends did this? It was awkward. It was weird. It was clumsy. But that's usually how it goes when you set your first boundary. What I have since learned about boundaries is while you never have to give a reason to say no, you most definitely do have to give a reason if you are cancelling. The best thing is, the more you get used to saying no, the less you have to cancel.

The good news is that we aren't learning boundaries for the first time, we are actually relearning them. Most children know where their boundaries stand. A baby communicates boundaries by screaming. Put them in the arms of a stranger and you will see a baby communicate when their physical boundaries are being crossed. With toddlers, as soon as they learn the word "no", they will use it liberally. Take his toy and my one-year-old nephew will yell "no" until I give it back. They might not have the full vocabulary to engage in a conversation, but they make that boundary clear.

At some point, we are taught by other people that our needs aren't as important as others. This could be a parent continuing to tickle you even though you have told them to stop, or being told to stop crying because it's impolite. My earliest memory of having my boundaries crossed was when I was around 10 and my family and I went to Santa Barbara to stay with a family friend for two weeks. The first night we arrived, he cooked this incredible meal for all of us and when it was time for dessert, he brought out this gorgeous berry tart. The only problem is I hate fruit. Yes, all fruit. Fruit triggers my gag reflex in quite an extreme way, so when he went inside to get a knife, I told my mum that I couldn't eat it. In my mind I debated, what's worse, telling him that I don't like fruit or potentially throwing up after a mouthful? My mum responded, "Just have a bite. He has spent all day making it, it's rude if you don't eat it." This is a comment that probably all mums make at some point. But what actually lies underneath this is the message that in order to be polite, I needed to disregard my own needs.

In fact, if we actually look at the situation, how would it be rude to tell him that I didn't like fruit? He couldn't have known and it's not that I am taking personal offence at his berry tart specifically. There would have been three other people around the table who would have enjoyed it and it would not have gone to waste. Intentional or not, I was being taught that my discomfort was unimportant and that the potential of upsetting another outweighed my own feelings.

Another reason why boundaries become harder to set as we grow older is due to our evolving Theory of Mind. Theory of Mind is a term used by psychologists to describe the skill of having awareness of your thoughts and the ability to think about both your beliefs and someone else's. When we are born, we are naturally very egocentric. As we develop, we realize that not only do we think, but others have thoughts too, and that some of those thoughts are about us. Suddenly it becomes more complicated to prioritize ourselves. A large portion of this is due to our need to be liked. Since we have a greater perception of what the other person is thinking, believing and assuming about us, the decisions that adults make and the behaviour that follows is much more guided by other people. But when we exchange being liked for lowering our boundaries, the unexpected result is not only a lack of respect but a rise in our own negative emotions from anger to resentment. People who accept that being disliked is a part of life are more willing to prioritize themselves and that is why boundaries are a crucial part of self-love.

The most common response I get when I teach boundaries is that this process is "easier said than done" and yes, I agree with you. Everything is easier said than done. If boundaries were easy, everyone would be setting them and there would be no need for this book. This phrase also comes from a victim mentality of believing that every other person in the world who is setting boundaries has always found it easy, and that you are the only person in the world who finds this difficult – but you are wrong. The reason this book exists is because people struggle to establish boundaries. Even though they are now a normal part of my life, they were once hard for me too. There is no promise in this book that any part of this will be easy, but it is simple: do you want to keep living your life the way you are or are you ready for something better? If you aren't, put the book down now and come back to it when you are ready. Some people need to reach their breaking point in order to be motivated to change. When you are ready, this book will be there for you, but if you are going to spend the rest of this book saying, "easier said than done", then you are wasting your time. Boundaries are really scary to set when you aren't used to them, but over time they become your norm. My hope is that by the end of this book, these changes will become a part of your daily life.

What Is a Boundary?

At their very core, boundaries are the way we teach others to treat us. They are how we communicate what is acceptable and what is not. They define where you end and another person begins. We need boundaries in order to protect ourselves from manipulation, gaslighting, disrespect and abuse.

Boundaries between you and others are like a house. Inside the house is your life, and the four walls that create the house are your protection from the outside world. You aren't completely closed off because you can open the door to let people in, but you only open that door when it is your choice. If someone were to kick the door down, that would feel like a violation – you wouldn't then tell them, "Oh well, since you are here, make yourself at home." That's the same as someone violating your boundary and you saying, "Well, since you are going to do what you want anyway, who am I to say anything about it?" If someone climbed through your window, you wouldn't let them in because that window was closed for a reason. If I didn't want to do something, my friends knew that if they pestered the old me long enough, I would give in. That's the same as someone knocking on your door all day and then you eventually letting them in simply so they stop annoying you. You would never do that!

Your home, like your life, is your space. You get to decide who comes in and who has to leave at any moment. If someone walked into your house and took a delicate vase and threw it on the ground, you would kick them out. Now imagine that the vase is a private, vulnerable piece of information.

— 13 —

How many times have you shared something confidential and it wasn't treated with the care it should have been? It is your house, and you get to decide what behaviour you tolerate inside it. Some people would allow others to wear shoes inside the house, while others don't like it. There are no right or wrong rules, but which are *your* rules? It's your house, they are your boundaries, and you decide.

Pia Mellody, a respected educator in the field of relationships, has previously described boundaries as "invisible and symbolic fences". She describes their purpose as three-fold:

1) To keep people from coming into our space and abusing us
2) To keep us from going into the space of others and abusing them
3) To give each of us a way to embody our sense of who we are

All three of these, and the third one in particular, allow us to form an identity that we have chosen that empowers us. This affects all areas of our life. You can have strong boundaries in one area of your life and weak boundaries in another. Identify the areas where you have the strongest boundaries and then use that as proof to yourself that you, just like everyone else, have successfully set boundaries before and have the ability to transfer those skills to other areas of your life.

Throughout this book, I give examples of how I have set boundaries and the language I used when doing so. Instead of telling you what your boundaries should be, I have found that the best way to teach this process is to share concrete examples from my own life. It is important to remember that these are my boundaries. Yours will not be the same as mine, in the same way your needs will not be the same as mine. The way you communicate may be different to the way I do, but these examples are to be used as an option and a starting point on how to phrase your own boundaries.

Throughout my time teaching boundaries, I am frequently asked, "Is my boundary unreasonable?", "Am I asking for too much?", "Is my boundary too needy?", all of them generally boiling down to "Am I allowed to set this boundary?" Personally, you are never going to hear me say that a boundary is too much or that you are unreasonable, demanding, high maintenance or selfish (in a negative way!) for asking for what you need. Not only because I think these are words that are largely only used against women who have needs, but also because I think it serves no purpose. Dismissing someone's needs does not stop that need from existing and at the end of the day, your boundaries are none of my business. Your needs are just that – yours. Your boundaries are just that – yours. The whole world can think you are overreacting and I will still believe you are allowed your feelings, your reactions and your boundaries. The other party might believe that your boundary is unreasonable, and they are allowed to think that and yet, it doesn't mean it actually is unreasonable. Instead of trying to determine if you are asking for too much, question if you are asking the right person. The right person respects your boundaries and will never make you feel like they are too much.

Do You Need More Boundaries in Your Life?

Here is a list of warning signs that you might need more boundaries. The more statements that are true, the more you struggle with boundaries – and all the more reason you need them in your life.

I find it hard to voice my opinions when I disagree with someone	True/False
People regularly talk about me behind my back	True/False
I struggle to say "no"	True/False
If someone is in a bad mood around me, my mood is affected	True/False
I find it difficult to end phone calls	True/False
I feel guilty when I ask for what I need	True/False
I have been described as passive-aggressive	True/False
I worry that if I don't agree with someone, their feelings will be hurt	True/False
I would rather everyone else be happy even if I am unhappy	True/False
If someone hurts my feelings, I will try to forget about it	True/False
My life is often full of drama	True/False
I replay conversations in my head after they have happened	True/False
When people fight around me, I feel like I have to fix it	True/False
I find it difficult to express anger and would rather stay silent	True/False

I work longer hours than the rest of my colleagues	True/False
I am the peacemaker in my family	True/False
I give more in my friendships than I get in return	True/False
I overshare when I feel uncomfortable or in new relationships	True/False
I value other people's opinions more than my own	True/False
I often feel resentment and I do not know how to express that	True/False
I am uncomfortable when the conversation is about me	True/False
I agree to things I don't want to do to keep the peace	True/False
I feel guilty when expressing my opinions	True/False
If another person has an incorrect opinion of me, I want to change it	True/False
When I tell people information in confidence, it is rarely kept private	True/False
I feel responsible for other people's happiness	True/False
I have relationships in my life that I would label as "toxic"	True/False
I am scared to be honest, in case it turns into an argument	True/False
People have described me as a "pushover" or "too nice"	True/False
I cannot trust the people in my life to be there for me	True/False
Other people in my life need me to be the strong, reliable one	True/False

Boundaries are essential for self-esteem, confidence and personal power. When you demand respect, your self-respect also flourishes. When you become more conscious of your needs and wants, your general self-awareness also increases. Boundaries grow your sense of self and allow you to build a strong identity. People with boundaries know what they want and who they are because the line between who they are and who the world wants them to be is clear.

We have become used to the idea that other people, namely our romantic partner, have a responsibility to look after us. Yet the idea that you should look after yourself seems bizarre to most people. Your self-care is your responsibility, and your responsibility only. Take care of yourself and you remove that job off other people's lists. In fact, write a list of all the things you expect your partner to do for you, whether it's keep you happy, make you feel beautiful or bring more excitement into your life, and ask yourself if you are fulfilling those requirements yourself. More likely than not, you aren't, and that's why you are looking for that in another person. Let's normalize fulfilling our own requirements. By doing so, our relationships will be healthier because we will be more self-sufficient.

There is a Jewish saying, "If I am not for myself, who will be for me?" (Ethics of the Fathers, 1:14). It is your responsibility to live your life for yourself. If you don't, who will? Think about the son who is going to medical school to make his parents happy and continue the family legacy of becoming doctors. Is that his goal or his parents'? Once he has achieved the goal of satisfying his parents, will the fulfilment from the job he never chose continue to satisfy him? And once his parents are gone, will he end up living with regrets? The problem is that most people let their lives be dictated by the expectations of others and rarely take the time to figure out what they want from their life, let alone how to achieve that.

If you remove the idea that being selfish means having a disregard for others, is there really a downside to selfishness? If you think of the most selfish person you know, you might recall times in your life when they've refused to do things that you want to do. It's annoying, but that annoyance is on you, not on them. Alternatively, you might be picturing a person who demands a lot of you, but is that person being selfish or are you not good at turning down their requests? A boundaried person would have no problem saying no, no matter how many times they are asked to do something they don't want to do. Are you picturing a person who is never there for you? Someone with healthy self-esteem would also not invest in a relationship where the effort wasn't reciprocated.

Another association with the word "selfish" is that a selfish person thinks the whole world revolves around them – but actually, that's just an insecure person. An insecure person assumes your silence is because you are annoyed at them, or interrupts a conversation to only talk about themselves. If we reframe the word "selfish" and realize that you have power in the way you respond to others, there are actually no downsides to prioritizing yourself. If the word "selfish" is one that makes you uncomfortable, or the concept of self-care makes you roll your eyes, then consider this book a guide on how to look after yourself.

The most challenging part of setting boundaries is that we often don't feel we deserve to set them. We don't believe our needs deserve to be met. Particularly if we have grown up where there was an absence of love, we spend our entire adulthoods chasing the attention we never got and will do anything and everything to attain that attention, no matter how much we have to ignore our own needs and desires. I see this a lot when I ask people to do homework after a coaching session; even if I say that it will only take five minutes, they will tell me that they don't have five minutes. Actually, you do, you've just decided you are not worth those five minutes. You have allocated them to someone else and deemed them more worthy of your time than yourself. Be more selfish.

Ultimately, we have to get you to start caring about yourself, first and foremost. I remember how scary that was for me initially. That first time I said no to going to that pub quiz, my mind jumped to the fact that my friend would be angry with me and then I asked myself if he would stop inviting me to everything. Because that's what the mind does, it exaggerates in order to scare you so that you stay safely in your comfort zone. But all those thoughts were about my friend – and if I was going to break this pattern, I needed to start thinking a little more about me. How did I *actually* feel? In a word, relieved. I was tired. I had worked all day and the last thing I wanted to do was leave the house. I had done what I wanted that evening and aside from the niggling thoughts of self-doubt, that made me happy.

To build up your self-esteem, it is time to learn what you have the right to ask for. It is important to know how you deserve to be treated and what you will accept so that you refuse to settle. This is the beginning of a list that you might want to complete yourself:

I have the right to:
- Be spoken to with respect
- Prioritize my needs and interests
- Have my feelings
- Communicate my thoughts
-
-
-
-
-
-
-
-
-
-
-
-

Myths Around Boundaries

There are a lot of misunderstandings around boundaries and we must clear these up from the outset.

Boundaries are mean

Boundaries in themselves are not mean. However, you might be communicating them in a way that could be perceived as mean. In which case, the problem is not the boundary but that you do not have the vocabulary to set boundaries in a kind way. If boundaries are set correctly, they are often laid down out of love and respect for the relationship and a desire to keep it healthy and sustainable. There is a certain level of vulnerability that is required to communicate these needs. Now that I have a broad understanding of boundaries, I am actually grateful when someone tells me directly that I have crossed their boundaries rather than sitting in resentment and releasing it in passive-aggressive comments.

Boundaries are walls

The person with no boundaries is interchangeable with the person who has walls up. They are two sides of the same coin. As Pia Mellody explains in her book *The Intimacy Factor*:

"If you have no boundaries to contain yourself, you are a spewer. You feel you can do anything you damn well please – like a god without accountability. If you have walls to contain yourself, you are rigid. You become shut down, one-up, judgemental and controlling. You become an oppressive god: "Sit down, shut up. I know what you need to do". Boundary work teaches us to modify these extremes."

Both are protection mechanisms to keep the person safe and for them to avoid being abandoned. The middle ground between the two is a person with boundaries, and this is where healthy lies. Walls and boundaries are completely different. Walls close you off from the world and prevent intimacy, whereas boundaries allow for healthier relationships and enable people to feel vulnerable while also staying safe. The intention behind putting up a wall is to keep a person out. The intention behind a boundary is to know the difference between me and you. Simply put, boundaries keep the people you want out, and walls keep everyone out. People who build walls have more in common with people with weak boundaries than meets the eye. They are two versions of the same insecurity: a fear of rejection and abandonment. One protects themselves by closing themselves off to everyone so they are always in the position of perceived power, and another protects themselves by trying to get everyone to like them by never saying no, and thus avoiding conflict. The latter has the idea that the more they can do for a person, the greater the chance that person won't leave.

Walls	Boundaries
Prevent relationships from forming and close you off from the world	Allow for healthier relationships
Prevent intimacy and closeness	Allow vulnerability in a safe environment
The intention is to keep people out	The intention is to know the difference between me and you
Keep everyone out	Keep the people you want out
Created out of fear and anger	Created out of love and respect
"Fuck me over and you are dead to me"	"Fuck me over and I'm not going to let it happen again"

Setting a boundary is the same as holding a grudge

These are quite separate concepts, but the reason why a lot of people confuse grudges and boundaries is because they are only accustomed to toxic relationship dynamics, so are confused when someone creates and consistently enforces boundaries. The difference is that grudges relate to forgiveness, whereas boundaries are about your treatment. Grudges are formed out of a desire to punish the receiving party and an inability to let an issue go. The reason grudges are often brought into the conversation of boundaries is because the receiving party believes that in order to be forgiven, the event needs to be forgotten completely.

Our society often gives us the message that we should forgive regardless of what has happened and whether the person is truly apologetic. They say just two words – "I'm sorry" – and you are expected to undergo an automatic, immediate process where all negative emotions dissipate; if you are unable to do this, then you are being bitter. I believe an apology should be given as a gift, not in exchange for forgiveness. Harriet Lerner discusses this in her book *Why Won't You Apologize?*, where she states she disagrees with the well-intentioned but potentially harmful idea that:

> ... forgiveness is the only path to a life that's not mired down in bitterness and hate and those who do not forgive the unapologetic offender are less spiritually evolved persons at greater risk for emotional and physical problems.

A grudge by definition is a persistent feeling of ill will or resentment resulting from a past insult or injury. It is that ill will and resentment that is the only part that is important to heal. When we discuss forgiveness, I don't think it is always imperative to forgive someone, but it is important you process all the negative feelings in your body. Whether it's anger or resentment, those emotions in your body are what will continue to hurt you. The ability to sit with them and feel them for long enough that they disappear is the crucial bit, not whether you forgive the person or even if you let them back in your life.

When a person sets a boundary, there is no ill will for the receiving party, unlike with a grudge. A boundary is about you and how you want to be treated, a grudge is about them and how they need to be punished. It is only when you can't communicate boundaries, that grudges are used out of the resentment that needs to be relieved.

Boundaries are made out of anger

Some of the time when boundaries are set, people make the assumption that you are angry with them. This is their own projection. Either they don't understand boundaries or they would be angry if they were in your situation. If you are setting boundaries out of anger, then you are doing it wrong and you need to take some space to process your own emotions before setting the boundary. If they are done correctly, boundaries are stated as a fact and not as an emotional reaction to a situation. They are stated in an emotionally neutral way, in the same tone you would reply if someone asked you your phone number.

We have to remember that most people have weak boundaries and have no awareness of it. Think of a child who has no boundaries their whole life. The first time a parent sets a boundary, it might be a little confusing for that child and the child might think their parents are angry with them.

Boundaries are permanent

Some boundaries are permanent, but not all need to be. The majority are flexible. You can have firm boundaries and you can also have flexible ones. A firm boundary in my online life is that I do not share information about my family on my public Instagram page. I believe this is important because I chose to have a more public life, and they did not agree to that. A flexible boundary in my online life is around my love life. When I first started posting online, my boundary was that I never talked about my love life. In the last couple of years, that boundary has shifted since my first book came out. My first book details how I lost my virginity and my first few experiences of dating. I chose to share this because I believed it was a pivotal part of my story, and since my first book was a memoir, it felt incomplete not to include it, so I changed my boundary. Now, I will share occasional experiences and snippets of my love life but I still won't share names or pictures of anyone I am dating or answer any questions about my love life. If I get into a long-term relationship, I may want to change this boundary again and it is my right to. You are allowed to change your mind and you are allowed to change your boundaries. They are yours, after all.

Different Types of Boundaries

Material boundaries

This includes your property and your belongings. Very early on, we often learn this with siblings who borrow our things without asking or when our parents enter our room without our permission.

Example of weak material boundaries

I grew up in a boarding school, and a frequent material boundary that was crossed was when someone lost their textbook, they would just take another person's off the shelf in order to not get in trouble. They would rarely give it back in time, and then the person whose book they had taken would get in trouble instead.

Example of strong material boundaries

In university, I shared a house with four girls and among the girls, I had the largest perfume collection. When we would get ready, the girls would often come to use one of my perfumes. I had no problem with that, but they all knew that there was one perfume they were not allowed to touch for sentimental reasons. They never asked why and never pressured me to let them give it a sniff. They simply accepted that and would use one of the others.

Physical boundaries

This is your body and your personal space. This can involve touching, hugging or even standing too close to you.

Examples of weak physical boundaries

In 2019, Joe Biden, former Vice President of the United States and, at the time, the Democratic nominee for the 2020 presidential election, was under scrutiny after allegations that people felt uncomfortable about how he had touched them, by kissing the back of their head or rubbing noses with them. It became part of the growing #MeToo conversation, but it should also be a part of the evolving conversation around boundaries. In his apology, he echoed this:

> I shake hands, I hug people, I grab men and women by the shoulders and say, 'You can do this.' Whether they are women, men, young, old, it's the way I've always been. It's the way I show I care about them, that I listen. Social norms have begun to change, they've shifted. And the boundaries of protecting personal space have been reset. And I get it. I get it. I hear what they're saying, I understand it. And I'll be much more mindful. That's my responsibility and I'll meet it.

What he is saying here is that when he wants to be encouraged, he likes it when people hug him or grab him by the shoulders to motivate him and therefore he made the classic human mistake of assuming everyone in the world thinks like this and would react like he would. But you should never assume others like to be supported in the same way you would. What you might love, another person might hate, and in order to know how best to help, all you have to do is ask.

Example of strong physical boundaries

The opposite to the above is the person who asks permission before they touch you. The above situation could be easily solved with a simple "Can I hug you?" before hugging someone. Similarly, parents with good physical boundaries also teach their kids good physical boundaries. We've often seen parents very innocently say, "Give your auntie a hug", but if good physical boundaries were in place, they can just as easily say, "Do you want to give your auntie a hug?" With this rewording, they are passing on the message that the child is allowed to decide what feels comfortable for them, in their own body, and that it is their choice. More importantly, if the child says no, it is important to respect that and not punish them for being "rude". If you give a child a choice, it is important to also respect the answer.

Emotional boundaries

Enacting emotional boundaries means knowing which emotions belong to me and which belong to you, and refusing to take responsibility for any emotions you don't own. With this also comes the realization that no one can *make* you feel anything. Assume responsibility for your own feelings and stop blaming other people for the emotions that you hold.

Examples of weak emotional boundaries

Have you ever met a person who, when they are in a bad mood, everyone else must join them? They will start picking fights and causing issues that are irrelevant to the initial situation, simply because if they can't be happy, no one else can. This is an example of weak emotional boundaries. They can also look like: guilting someone to get your own way, trying to make someone else responsible for your emotions, or manipulating someone in order to relieve your own negative emotions. A lack of emotional boundaries often comes with a lack of self-awareness and this often results in people projecting their negative emotions from one area of their life onto a completely separate situation. Common examples of this are road rage or people who take their anger out on waiters. The anger is never really about the food or the traffic, but because they have unresolved anger in another area of life, they are transferring it to an individual in a setting where they are less likely to suffer repercussions for their anger (like a waiter) or perceived victimless situations (like road rage, at least if your windows are up).

Examples of strong emotional boundaries

Knowing what emotions belong to you and which do not is crucial. I teach this distinction often in relation to body shame and a sentence that I often tell my clients to use is, "That is your shame, it doesn't belong to me." This works with every other emotion as well. One of the people who took this sentence and applied it to their own life was being body shamed by her mum. In this instance, her mum was using her upcoming wedding as a tool to body shame her by saying that she will be ashamed if she walks down the aisle at her size. She turned to her mum and calmly stated, "No, *you* would be ashamed to walk down the aisle at my size. That is your shame, that doesn't belong to me. I am very excited to walk down the aisle in my body." I often describe it as if someone is holding a bag of shame and asking you, "Hey! Can you carry this for me?" – and people accept it without even looking inside it. If you looked in the bag, you would turn it down instantly and hand it back to them. And that's exactly what this woman did – she handed the shame back and had fun on her wedding day.

Intellectual boundaries

Intellectual boundaries include ideas and thoughts as well as our conversational and time boundaries. Being able to communicate without being dismissive of another person's opinions, apologizing when appropriate and allowing for disagreements to happen without them evolving into arguments are a great sign of intellectual boundaries. When it comes to time, good time boundaries mean showing up when you say you are going to and communicating when you are running late. That means none of this texting, "I'm five minutes away" when you are still in the shower.

Examples of weak intellectual boundaries

Those with weak intellectual boundaries will be unable to separate their thoughts and opinions from the people around them. They find it difficult to "agree to disagree". An example of this is when a parent won't accept that their child does not hold the same religious or spiritual beliefs and they impose their own religion. If a child chooses a different religion or decides to be an atheist, and the parent is unable to respect their choice and dismisses their beliefs, these are a sign of weak intellectual boundaries.

Examples of strong intellectual boundaries

Being on the internet every day means I open myself up to criticism daily. I take it on board, consider it and then decide how to change my behaviour to make myself a better person. However, if criticism is attached to a personal attack, the criticism is dismissed. Being able to communicate your disagreement with someone without personal abuse is vital in healthy communication and if a comment comes with personal abuse in any capacity, whether it is a valid criticism or not, I do not engage and instead block the person.

Sexual boundaries

These are your boundaries in a sexual context and while the majority of these will be physical, it can also include the words used in a bedroom context. The most notable examples of these boundaries being crossed would include sexual assault and rape, but it is important to note that when it comes to consent, that really is the bare minimum of sexual boundaries. Within that consent, we must be conscious of coercion or pressure to consent. When it comes to verbal boundaries, not only are safe words important but in the most healthy relationships, there will also be a conversation around which words your partner(s) do and don't like, both in the bedroom and in the medium of sexting.

Examples of weak sexual boundaries

One of the prime examples of this is unsolicited dick pics, but this also could be as simple as someone refusing to take no for an answer. It could be a long-term partner who has always wanted to try a sexual act that you are not interested in, and they hope that their persistent nagging will lead to your boundaries coming down. In that case, both parties would have weak sexual boundaries. If you oblige in doing things you don't want to do, either to be liked or out of fear you will be rejected, then you also have weak sexual boundaries.

Examples of strong sexual boundaries

On the reality television show, *Love Island*, the couples often get a chance to sleep in a separate room called The Hideaway, away from the other contestants. This allows them more privacy and stereotypically, they "do bits" when they are in that room. In Season 6, Siânnise and Luke get this opportunity. Once in the room, Siânnise gives Luke a lap dance. Before any more happens, Luke asks, "Can I touch you?" before placing his hands around her waist. It led to Luke being praised as a "consensual King", but is a great sign of strong sexual boundaries that he didn't see a lap dance or lingerie as automatic consent to be touched.

Why Boundaries Go Wrong

When I started telling people I was writing a book about boundaries, I received a number of mixed reactions, the most shocking of which was people asking me what boundaries were. This was not because they didn't know how to set them, but because they were second nature to these people, and therefore didn't need a label. Almost like how a person who learns English as their first language would not be able to tell you what the pluperfect tense is, but a person learning English as a second language has to learn the terminology to go with it because it's a foreign concept. It's the same with boundaries. There is a percentage of the population that, upon the mention of boundaries, responds with, "But that's common sense" or "Don't we all do that?" But no, unfortunately, we don't and the difference often comes down to trauma and childhood. The woman who taught me everything I know about boundaries, my life coach Michelle Zelli, happens to be an expert in it, and trauma work is her speciality. So when it comes to explaining how boundaries go wrong, she's the best person I know to explain the background behind it.

The Relationship Between Trauma and Boundaries:
An Explainer by Michelle Zelli

Our boundaries are created by our family blueprint. We absorb what we see as children, which in turn soon becomes our own way of being. When I meet most of my clients, they have trauma. Some are aware of it, but others are not, instead believing they are not normal and need fixing. One of the many consequences of trauma and living a boundaryless life is that we believe there is something intrinsically wrong with us because our emotions roller-coaster between extremes, feeling so deeply one day and being completely numb to our emotions the next. But I'd like to set the record straight: there is nothing wrong with my clients, and there is nothing wrong with you. This was your coping mechanism to be able to grow up in a home that didn't feel safe. You adapted to the environment that was your home.

If, as children, we feel misunderstood or have a lack of perceived safety, our nervous system tends to be on high alert for danger at every corner. It is working overtime to protect you and keep you safe. This hypervigilance is often carried throughout our lives, constantly scanning for potential threats and indications that we are bad, crazy or simply not good enough. This creates high reactivity and this traumatic environment, in turn, leaves us with an inability to trust ourselves and others. We are navigating life without a reliable compass, which is designed to inform us as to what's our stuff and what's theirs, and the result is that you think everything is your fault. This is evidence of the underlying trauma you are left with. By definition, a person suffering trauma responses has usually been the victim of weak or tyrannical boundaries by their parental figures in their formative years.

Having a challenging childhood like the one I describe above creates a certain toughness, a resilience. It often leads to us arming ourselves with an exterior designed to protect us by walling off and shutting down, creating a perceived coldness. Many traumatized adults become unable to tolerate human connection and find ourselves pushing people away. The intention of these carefully crafted walls is to keep our deeply sensitive insides safe, but instead our weak (or what I like to call "leaky") boundaries mean we alternate between bringing down the walls and allowing (or even inviting!) people to do whatever they want to us. We hurl ourselves from one unsafe connection to another and yet the most painful connection we hold is the one we have with ourselves. When we're hurt, our boundaries become walls; when we're needy, they become mush. We alternate between the two – walls and no boundaries at all – unable to find the middle ground that we were never taught. I call these two extremes the Devil and the Doormat.

The Doormat allows people to walk all over them. While pandering to other people's needs, they feel resentful, angry and powerless to change, but the behavioural dance trots on. Scared of rejection and judgement, the Doormat puts other people before themselves and withers into a slow demise.

Unless, that is, they get sick of being taken for a ride, at which point our Doormat will often do a full 180-degree flip and channel their inner Devil. The Devil does not care about other people's boundaries or needs. Now the person who was previously the Doormat becomes walled off and tooled up. Nobody can get close; they are defensive, conflict-ready and often find themselves misunderstood, alone and sad. By going too far with this flip-flop, they are now proving to themselves that their thoughts ("I'm a horrible person" and "Whatever's going on is all my fault") are true. This inconsistency is exhausting, not only for the person living this life, but also for others around them who have to experience these constant flips. This is because we don't know how we feel and were never given the room to figure it out.

"Enmeshment" is a term first used by Salvador Minuchin, a pioneer in Structural Family Therapy. When a family dynamic dictates that all members of the family think, feel and believe the same things, there is little wiggle room for individuality. These largely unspoken rules mean that healthy interaction is off the table, and we're unable to distinguish between our own emotions and those of the person we're interacting with. An enmeshed human often feels "'odd'" outside the family system – and if you dare to be different within it, you will get labelled the family "black sheep", with the potential for being rejected, mocked and judged. In these situations, your emotional state becomes dependent on how the other person is feeling and behaving, and you lose yourself in the belief that you alone are responsible for their feelings and behaviour. Enmeshed people often feel that it's their job to make everything go smoothly for everyone else, and in the process sacrifice themselves and their needs, wants and self-esteem.

In other family systems, an entire family can revolve around a narcissist. The narcissist must have their needs met, primarily to make them feel good. Because they sadly lack self-esteem, narcissists take whatever they need to feel "special" from other people. They are covering up a primal wound of feeling worthless and undeserving of love. In order to overcorrect inner worthlessness, they need to be acknowledged as the biggest, the best, the boldest. To protect themselves, they build a flash and formidable veneer for the world – often in the form of success, trinkets and bluster – but the ultimate aim is for them to appear and feel superior. Narcissists need you to provide their good feelings about themselves, and your needs are of no consideration. Without boundaries, you are a natural target for the narcissist because you are an endless fountain of "giving". They will continue to take and take, with no consideration or remorse about the fact that it's to the detriment of your own life and self-esteem.

No matter which type of family you grew up in, learning boundaries in adulthood is essential, especially when you weren't taught them in childhood. Boundaries mean you will be protected from either a narcissist looking to take advantage or an enmeshed family where you seem to be fielding never-ending opinions about your life and invasions to your privacy. In my own life, boundaries have saved me from love addiction, drug addiction, adult family abuse, health issues and so much more. They have created a courage and ballsiness that have turned my life into the greatest gig imaginable. I do what I love, how and when I choose, with great people. Without committing to the mastery of boundaries, I would not be able to trust myself to deliver on my goals, nor protect myself from familiar adversaries: distraction, despair and destruction.

Within family structures, many of us didn't have our needs met in childhood – we were shown that our needs were unimportant when they were dismissed, overlooked or misunderstood. In order to reverse this belief, and master boundaries, we must stop accepting crumbs from the table and instead start understanding ourselves and what we need to be our best. I call it self-mastery, and it is the most exciting ride life can offer. When we get to know ourselves, we reject the crumbs and ask for the à la carte menu. We get choice, freedom and start to design the life that we want, not the life that everyone else wanted for us.

The first step is to realize that anger occurs when we are not having our needs met. Getting to know yourself means acknowledging this anger and asking yourself what you need. Within this book, Michelle will give you the wisdom you need to start implementing boundaries, but it must begin with your determination to ask for your needs to be met.

When it comes to making change, there are three kinds of people: those who sit up and pay attention to the first tickle of the feather; those who wait until the metaphorical brick sails through their window; and those who wait until the brick is a bus, watching over and over again as their life implodes, failing to learn the lessons. These warning signs and tests will keep appearing until we present the proof that we've had enough, in the form of our own changed behaviour. Take a moment to look back down your timeline – do you act when the feather shows up, or wait for the bus to crash into your world?

These opportunities are presented in many different ways, perhaps as a crush who doesn't call despite a promise to do so, or a friend who "forgets" her wallet yet again. Start seeing these challenges as a chance to test your new boundaries and the opportunities will keep coming until you've proved that you've learned the lesson. It's a great journey you are embarking on – the world needs more healthy boundaries and that change starts right here!

– Michelle Zelli, Executive Life Coach (@MichelleZelli)

INTRODUCTION

CHAPTER 2:

THE BARRIERS TO BOUNDARY SETTING

There are a number of things that stand in the way of us setting boundaries, so it is imperative that we look at the obstacles standing in our way. Most people will be quick to say they can't set boundaries, but if they were asked why, they would draw a blank. If you are able to pinpoint where your difficulty with boundaries lies, we are able to change it. These obstacles fit into six categories.

1) You Don't Know What You Want

Without boundaries, we find it challenging to figure out who we are and what we want. We merge with the people around us, and the desires they have for our life often become our own desires. To know what you want from your life, you need to know your values.

2) You Don't Know How You Feel

When you are not clear on what is yours and what is another person's, it becomes easy to carry their emotions and be unclear about which feeling belongs to which person. You can only process emotions that belong to you, so if you are carrying someone else's, you need to become aware of that.

3) You Don't Know How to Process What You Feel

We hear the phrase "process your feelings" a lot, but what is rarely taught is how to *feel* your feelings. Understanding that emotions sit inside our body and learning to bring our attention to those sensations is the key to being able to let them go. Emotions are designed to be temporary; it is the inability to process them that keeps the energy stuck in our body.

4) You Don't Know How to Set Boundaries

Learning how to communicate boundaries is like learning how to speak a new language. With beginners, the first reaction to being given the tools to communicate boundaries is "I can't say that", but you can! You just haven't before. You are entering unknown and unfamiliar territory and it is OK to feel uncomfortable. You are not used to boundaries and unaccustomed to the reactions that people will have. Similarly, they will be unaccustomed to you standing up for yourself.

5) Guilt After Setting Boundaries

The first few times you set boundaries, it is likely that you will feel guilty afterwards. After all, it goes against everything you have been taught. It will take time for your self-esteem to build for you to realize that you deserve to be treated better, and boundaries are going to ensure that that happens.

6) Fear of Being Disliked

A person without boundaries has a life that is often dictated by others' opinions, including operating in a way that avoids negative reactions. This is impossible. Another person's opinion is out of your control. As long as you prioritize their opinions, you will continue to struggle to set boundaries because boundaries will make you less likeable.

While being aware of these barriers is a huge step in being able to overcome them, they won't be conquered simply by reading this book. It's important you take your learnings and apply them to your life. Within life coaching, we call this "taking action", so throughout the book there will be Take Action steps that you can do to either change your mentality or create a behaviour change in your life. A lot of these will require you to write something down. As much as you'll be tempted to do it in your head, writing it down makes you more likely to actually create the change. Not only does this force you to spend longer on the exercise, but it also engages more areas of your brain so that you are more likely to commit the action to memory.

1) You Don't Know What You Want

Before boundaries, I could not have told you what I wanted in life. If you asked me what I wanted in a partner, I would have been shocked I had a choice. I only ever thought about if they liked me – I never considered if I liked them back. When it came to my career, I could give you a job title I wanted, but in terms of the actual day-to-day of what my work life would consist of, I would draw a blank. If you asked me what I was looking for in life, I would have replied, "To be happy" – but that's not realistic. No one is happy all day, every day. It is unattainable. I wanted to be happy but I didn't know what made me happy.

The key to understanding how we tick as humans is to understand our values. These principles lie behind every decision we make and drive our behaviours. Values also explain why we make choices in some areas of life more easily than in others: we have a distinct set of values for each area. Most people aren't consciously aware of their values, but their choices are nonetheless guided by these deeply held beliefs. But to be in the driver's seat of your own life, it's time to be conscious of what's important to you.

What is a value?

Values are intangible higher-level generalizations that help navigate our decisions and are sometimes called criteria. For example, if you were to ask someone what they value in health and fitness and they replied with "running". Running is not a value but if you were to ask "What does running give you?" and they said "a sense of achievement", then achievement is the value. They are usually one-word answers that categorize a number of things. Essentially, it's what we value in life. (The only exception to the intangible rule is money, because it symbolizes a lot more in society.) Examples of values include:

- Respect
- Security
- Authority
- Love
- Sex
- Fun
- Excitement
- Understanding
- Loyalty
- Accomplishment

What are your values?

Now it's your turn. In order to elicit your values, you need to ask yourself: "What is important to me in my _____?" Fill in the gap with the specific area of life, such as: "What is important to me in my career?" Get a piece of paper and write out all the life areas and corresponding values you can think of, until you run out. Then it's time to order them. To help get the order right, ask yourself, "If I could only have one thing on this list, which would it be?" and then ask, "If

I had _____, but not _____, would I be happy?". So you might have a question like, "If I had romance in my love life, but not sex, would I be happy?" Reorder them until you have a complete list and fill in your final eight.

An important note

This is an exercise that you may want to revisit every year or so. Values change, just as our priorities change. It is worth noting that the word you chose won't have the same meaning for everybody else. For example, if I say authority is really important to me in my career, that could mean that I want to be heard and listened to by my team. To another person, authority could mean being seen as an authority in your industry. It doesn't matter that there are differences between people, but it's important that you realize that two words that seem similar in your head could hold different connotations, such as success and accomplishment.

Have you ever had a moment where you have felt really angry and you don't know why? Anger is a sign your boundaries have been crossed and your values list will now give you clues as to why that is the case. For example, if you and your parents get into a fight where they believe your sister over you, it may be difficult to put your finger on what has specifically annoyed you. However, if your top value in the area of family and friends is being understood, then that explains it. Now when you set boundaries, you can communicate that you felt misunderstood.

Take Action: There are three areas of your life below, to get you started on prioritizing your values. But you should complete this exercise for any areas of your life that you deem important, and specifically those in which you lack boundaries. Other areas might include health and fitness, financial life, social life or spirituality – use the fourth space to explore values in another area of your life.

Career
1) _____
2) _____
3) _____
4) _____
5) _____
6) _____
7) _____
8) _____

Love life
1) _____
2) _____
3) _____
4) _____
5) _____
6) _____
7) _____
8) _____

Family & Friends
1) _____
2) _____
3) _____
4) _____
5) _____
6) _____
7) _____
8) _____

....
1) _____
2) _____
3) _____
4) _____
5) _____
6) _____
7) _____
8) _____

2) You Don't Know How You Feel

Figuring out which emotions aren't yours

Many people with weak boundaries have issues with co-dependency. The definition of a co-dependent, according to Melody Beattie in her book *Codependent No More*, is: "A codependent person is one who has let another person's behaviour affect him or her [or them], and who is obsessed with controlling that person's behaviour."

Co-dependency is a learned behaviour that occurs when a child is raised without adequate boundaries and without enough love and attention. This behaviour, though learned in childhood, continues into adulthood as the child learns that if they do more for others, their usefulness will hopefully result in a reciprocation of love and affection. This leads to the person doing a lot of caretaking of people who are not their responsibility. A symptom of that caretaking is that the co-dependent feels responsible for other people's emotions, experiences anxiety and guilt when others have negative emotions and feels it is their responsibility to both carry the other person's emotional burdens and fix the problem at hand.

An example of this is if a co-dependent's partner has fallen out with a friend, the person experiences emotions as if it is their own friendship that is going through difficulties. While empathy is normal in a situation like this, you should not be experiencing those emotions to the same extent as your partner is. When you do everything for someone else, there is an implicit assumption that they are not capable of looking after themselves. We cannot protect people from their own emotions. If you do the hard work for them, you actually do that person a disservice in not giving them the ability to process their own emotions themselves. Stop doing their emotional work for them. Empathy is a great skill, but if your empathy is so extreme that you absorb the energy of the room, then you are going to be left feeling depleted. Your own emotions are enough to deal with, and feeling other people's feelings is not your responsibility. Doing so takes away their power. Even if you think you are doing them a favour, you are actually preventing them from ever gaining independence.

If you are unsure if the feelings you hold actually belong to you, ask yourself if the stimulus happened in your life or someone else's. Are you in a room where someone is experiencing an intense reaction? Taking a physical step back and a deep breath and simply asking yourself if this feeling belongs to you should clarify it, but if not, we need to enhance your self-awareness. Get a pen and paper and note down times in your life when you have experienced someone else's emotion. Once you become aware of the times you have done it before, you will have a list of red flags to help indicate when you are doing it again.

No one can make you feel anything

How many times have you heard a person say, "She makes me so angry"? No one can *make* you feel anything. You will know this if you have ever tried to make someone feel guilty for something for which they are completely unapologetic. No matter how hard you try, a person who doesn't care can't be made to. Your emotions are important and how you feel is valid but unfortunately, the moment that energy exchange happens, those emotions become yours and are your responsibility to manage and process.

Let's take an example of your father eavesdropping on your phone conversation with your boyfriend. When you hang up the phone and realize he has invaded your privacy, you are angry. The eavesdropping was the stimulus, the response is anger and your reaction might be to yell or storm out of the room. It is easy to think that the jump from stimulus to response to reaction is automatic, but it isn't. If it was your sister eavesdropping, your response might be different. If it was a stranger on the train eavesdropping, your response might be complete apathy. Realizing there is space between the stimulus and response means you have more control over your reaction as well. Understanding that your response doesn't need to have a reaction is another part of owning your power. Furthermore, it is critical in the realization that the emotions you have aren't negative, but your reaction to the emotion might be negative. For example, anger is a healthy emotion, but throwing a chair across the room is not a healthy response.

It isn't what happened, it is the meaning you give it

What is going on internally between your stimulus and feeling, is your brain is creating meaning. Our brains are meaning-finding devices, and when there is an absence of facts, your brain will do what it needs to fill in the rest of the story. What we don't know, we make up and often, what we make up is worse than reality.

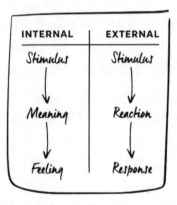

INTERNAL	EXTERNAL
Stimulus	Stimulus
↓	↓
Meaning	Reaction
↓	↓
Feeling	Response

Within coaching, we use the term "stories" a lot. It is important to be clear about what is fact and what is a story you are making up. To use the above example of your dad's eavesdropping, before you feel angry, your brain might be telling you that your dad doesn't care about your privacy or that your dad doesn't like your partner. You have directly correlated his behaviour to those two ideas and that is what creates the anger. If you let your negative thoughts spiral, it turns into a story that you tell yourself:

that no one cares about your needs, everyone treats you like a child and if it was your sister, no one else would be listening to her conversations. These are stories, not facts, and if you asked your dad why he was listening to your private conversation, it could be these things or it could be something else.

Alternatively, there are times when feelings arise but you do not act on them because of the meaning you assign to them. An example of this is when you feel fear in a movie cinema. Whilst you can feel it in your body, your brain assigns the meaning that you are safe and this is how you are meant to feel and therefore there is no response.

There is no such thing as a negative emotion

The way we discuss emotions from an early age is fundamentally flawed, and that starts with the initial idea that there are positive and negative emotions. There aren't. Emotions aren't good or bad – they exist, and we place our own judgements on them based on what we have been taught growing up. All emotions are natural, human and healthy. It's the way that we are taught to handle them that makes them unhealthy.

How we feel and how we act on our feelings are two distinct things. An emotion at its most basic form does not cause harm, but how we act on that emotion can cause harm. The reason most people think anger, of all the emotions, is the worst or most unhealthy one is because of what people do in anger. The emotion and how it is utilized are separate parts of the same process. The key to healthy anger is to ensure you get the physical energy out of your body, without actually hurting anyone or aiming it in anyone's direction. A few suggestions: punch a pillow, yell at a wall, write an angry letter but do not send it, or my personal favourite, singing along at full volume to angry songs.

Each emotion serves a purpose. Repressing it doesn't make the emotion disappear, but instead will make it manifest in another way, in another area of your life. If we were given the tools to cope properly with each emotion, we'd actually be able to move through them and allow them to have less control.

Anger: The most important emotion for boundary setting, anger is a clear sign your boundaries have been crossed, and it is the only "negative" emotion that creates energy. This creation of energy happens in order to provide you with the strength to protect your morals and values. Have you ever been exhausted and then something happens and you get angry? There is usually a resurgence of energy. Harriet Lerner puts it best in her book *The Dance of Anger*:

> Anger is neither legitimate nor illegitimate, meaningful nor pointless. Anger simply is. To ask, 'Is my anger legitimate?' is similar to asking, 'Do I have the right to be thirsty? After all, I just had a glass of water fifteen minutes ago. Surely my thirst is not legitimate. And besides, what's the point of getting thirsty when

I can't get anything to drink now, anyway?' Anger is something we feel. It exists for a reason and always deserves our respect and attention. We all have a right to everything we feel – and certainly our anger is no exception.

Fear: It is designed to protect you and warn you of what's ahead. The only problem is that sometimes your brain detects something which isn't dangerous and flags it as harmful. Fear will not hurt you but it will do its best to try to deter you from the action you are about to take. Its motive is to keep you safe and within your comfort zone and whilst that is helpful if a lion is going to eat you, it's not helpful in terms of personal growth and trying to do more with your life. We can listen to the fear, acknowledge that it is trying to keep us safe and then make a conscious decision about the choice we have in front of us.

Sadness: If you want to see how uncomfortable people are with sadness, all you need to do is cry, or bring up a conversation that might cause you to cry. In an instant, they'll jump in to say, "Don't cry", because they are so uncomfortable with their own sadness that seeing yours has the same effect on them.

Guilt: Guilt is the way our unconscious mind tells us that we have behaved in a way that isn't aligned with our values and who we want to be. More on guilt later.

Shame: Shame is actually just a derivative of guilt. Guilt is about behaviour, while shame is about your being. It is the difference between "I did something bad" and "I am bad".

Take Action: What emotions are you carrying that are not yours? Complete this writing prompt:

The [insert emotion] that I am carrying about [insert situation] does not belong to me. It belongs to [insert the name of the person it belongs to]. I release this emotion. It is not of me, or for me. This emotion is not my responsibility and serves no purpose in my life.

If you locate where that emotion sits in your body and say this aloud, it often helps to release the emotion. Breathe into that location in your body until it is fully released.

_____

_____

_____

_____

_____

_____

_____

_____

_____

_____

_____

3) You Don't Know How To Process What You Feel

We are never taught how to feel our feelings. In fact, if anything, we are taught the exact opposite. Children are born with a natural ability to feel and react to their emotions. It is the adults that surround them who project their own discomfort around their own feelings. This is often conveyed with comments such as "Don't cry", "Don't make a big deal about it" or "You think this is bad? Think about the children with no food." This invalidation of their emotions teaches the child to hold feelings in and not express themselves. As that child grows, they develop their own ways to diminish how they feel. At the time I am writing this, we are in the middle of the Covid-19 coronavirus pandemic, which has been a prime example of people not allowing themselves emotions. Instead, they remind themselves that there are people who have it worse than them, and as a result, they compound their sadness with guilt, preventing them from being able to process either emotion. In reality, their guilt doesn't improve anyone else's situation and being stuck in their compounded emotions just makes their situation harder.

I use the phrase "process your emotions" throughout the book, so let me expand on what I mean. In coaching, we refer to emotions as "energy in motion", and we need to get that energy out. The reason why we avoid processing is because if you put your focus on an emotion, the pain usually increases and this deters us from continuing to feel it. However, remember that if you do not feel it and do not process it, that feeling will stay inside of you. It will surface at inconvenient moments in smaller doses, in the form of projecting onto other people, and that ends up being more destructive than sitting with the pain for the length of time it needs. If you are able to work through it, you will find the feeling either softens or disappears completely. The more you incorporate this into your life, the less you project onto others.

First of all, we need to remove all judgement around our feelings. Often when our emotions don't make sense, we spend time compounding those emotions by building on top of them. For example, people get scared of their fear, or get angry that they are angry. Emotions don't need to make sense. When someone experiences grief, they often allow sadness – but if they feel angry, they then compound that emotion by feeling guilty that they are angry at a dead person. This will not allow you to process that emotion. You are allowed to be angry that someone died, no matter how irrational or illogical that is. When an emotion arises (and once you have figured out that it is your emotion to process and not someone else's), the three main things you need to remember are:

1) You are allowed to feel however you feel
2) Emotions are valid
3) It is safe to feel your emotions

You can remind yourself by writing this down – stick a Post-it note on your mirror, write a note in your phone, set it as your phone background or simply repeat all three as a mantra or even as a conversation to yourself. When I feel an intense rise in emotion, and I experience resistance in allowing myself to feel it, I will often say in my head:

> "You are safe. You are allowed to feel this emotion and what you are feeling right now is valid and important."

There will be times in my life when I don't have enough uninterrupted time to process my emotions and there are times when I do not feel safe enough to fall apart. Let's say I have public speaking tomorrow and I am experiencing sadness around a breakup. This is a moment where I would not feel safe enough to fall apart because I would worry that I would not be able to put myself back together for an important job the next morning. So, what I do in these moments is I schedule a time to be alone. My unconscious mind is then able to rest in the knowledge that it will be felt at the weekend, or as soon as I am able to, and this helps put those emotions to the back of my mind until I have the time to properly dedicate myself to processing what I need to feel. When I schedule time in to process my emotions, it shows my unconscious mind that my feelings are a priority. The action of creating time in my schedule, whether that's cancelling social events or simply writing it in my calendar, shows me that my feelings are valid and deserve my time.

On those days, I need to be alone because it allows me to remove the mask that we often present to the world. Solitude allows me to step back from the pressure of being a life coach, of being @ScarredNotScared – I can just be human and be Michelle. I believe it is vital that each individual knows how to comfort themselves; as much as the comfort, love and affection from others can soothe you, those don't actually resolve the emotions that are residing in your body.

The Process

The first thing to do is to find somewhere comfortable to sit, and surround yourself in blankets or light candles – whatever will make you feel soothed and safe. Make sure your feet are on the floor and take a deep breath. Breathe in through your nose for four seconds, hold it for four seconds and then breathe out through your mouth for six seconds. Do this a few times and then scan your body for any physical sensations. Is there an outstanding place of tension or pain? You might be experiencing it as heat or a tingling sensation, similar to pins and needles.

When you have located the physical sensation in your body, bring your awareness to it and focus on that feeling. The majority of the time, that feeling will intensify and it may even be painful. This is the pain that you have been suppressing. It is common for emotional pain to present as physical pain as your emotions are held in your body. The longer you keep your attention on it and continue to breathe into it, the tension or pain should ease off or sensations could migrate to a new area of your body. Follow that sensation wherever it goes. For example, if you were feeling a tension in your heart, you might feel it move up to your throat.

If thoughts come into your brain, either trying to assign an emotion to that sensation or trying to explain why you feel the way you do, bring your awareness back to the sensation in your body. There is no need to silence these thoughts, because by redirecting your attention to the feelings within your body, the inner voice will quiet down anyway. You might find that you feel the urge to shout or scream, especially if the sensation rises into your throat. If you are completely alone, allow yourself to do that. If you are not completely alone, grab a pillow and yell into it. This may seem strange, but your emotion wants to be expressed and as long as you are not hurting anyone around you, this is a healthy way to process it.

Similarly, if you are feeling a tingling sensation in your arms and legs, you might want to shake them as vigorously as you can. This is usually fear or trauma energy that is trapped in your body. If you feel a rise in anger, you might have the urge to punch something. I often get my squash racket and slam that into a pillow. Punching a pillow also works. In our society, an act like this would worry people because we see all forms of aggression as bad. But as long as that aggression is never directed at an individual (and that includes yourself), it allows the energy to be released in a similar way to a boxing class or a game of tennis. Dancing can also be a great release for both fear and angry energy in the body, but in order for it to be released, the emotion in question needs to be brought to your conscious awareness. That is what this exercise will do.

If you need to take a break because the sensations feel too intense, then do so, but the more you process your emotions with exercises like this, the more your tolerance grows and the more you become self-aware around when an emotion is rising.

Some people experience difficulty accessing their sadness, especially if they were punished for crying when they were younger, so you might need some material to provoke sadness. Any time I am experiencing a block in emotions, I go on YouTube and look at videos that are a part of the "Try Not To Cry" challenge. Once you start crying, it will be easier to release the rest of your sadness. Similarly, my go-to shows are *Grey's Anatomy* or *This Is Us* if I need a good cry. Movie-wise, *Marley & Me* tends to get me going. And if none of that works, I have a playlist of sad music on my phone. Once the emotion is triggered, focus back on your situation. You will not be processing the emotion if you continue thinking about the TV show or movie. Use it as a tool to open up but don't stay there. Return back to what you were processing.

Another key part of my journey of learning how to process my feelings was learning about the concept of the "inner child". The inner child is the child that lives within all of us, and if we were not given the safety, love or affection we needed growing up, our childhood wounds can resurface when we are an adult. Sometimes when emotions arise, particularly when they seem more intense than the situation warrants, it is usually because it is reminding you of a past event or feeling that was never healed as a child. This is often the case if you feel a huge sudden surge in emotion. If this happens, it is rarely about the situation in front of you, but about something from your past. For example, if your colleagues were excluding you at work and leaving you out of important decisions, it could remind you of past events in childhood when you felt rejected by your friendship group. While yes, some of your hurt or sadness will be about the situation at hand, the familiarity of this past hurt could make you regress and use your previous coping mechanisms, such as pushing people away or using passive-aggressive comments.

In order to communicate with your inner child, you again need to find a quiet place where you can be alone and make yourself as comfortable as possible. When you think of the situation that has brought up emotions, ask yourself:

- Is this feeling familiar?
- When was the first time I had a feeling similar to this?
- What age was I when it happened?

Trust your first instinct when you ask yourself these questions. Overthinking or overanalyzing will remove you from your emotions in an attempt to intellectualize the exercise. People do this out of fear, so if you find yourself doing this, ask yourself the question again and go for the first answer, even if it doesn't make sense to you and even if you can't remember the specific memory. Trust the age that first pops into your mind and visualize yourself at that age.

In the example of being excluded by your colleagues, that event could remind you of a specific situation when you were seven years old and you turned up to school and your best friend suddenly wasn't talking to you and you didn't know why, and then you went home and told your mum that it happened and she told you that it probably wasn't a big deal and that your friend was having an off day. This is not about blame, or your mum doing anything wrong or your best friend being a bad friend. This is about this feeling lingering inside you and the need for this feeling and this memory to be healed. As you picture that little seven-year-old version of you, you have the opportunity to parent her as the adult you are now. Sit her down and have a conversation. Listen to her and let her say what she wants to say to you. Maybe your inner child needs to hear that they are loved or that "adult you" is there to support them and will never leave them. The conversation could go something like this:

"I am sorry you are upset. I would be upset too if I was in your situation. I want you to know that I love you and that I am always going to be here for you, no matter what happens."

"What if she doesn't want to be my friend because I am a bad person?"

"You are not a bad person. You have not done anything wrong in this situation and you are a lovable person who deserves friends who will talk to you when they have an issue with you."

Allow that child's fears to arrive. Validate them and visualize giving her the love and support she deserved in that instant. Tears might arise – release them along with this energy of the past that has been stuck inside your body. There are also many inner child meditations that could help facilitate these conversations if you feel you need support. My most used one is Glenn Harrold's *Heal Your Inner Child* meditation, which comes as an audiobook.

Truly feeling your emotions prior to boundary setting lets you distance yourself from the heat of the situation and place boundaries in a firm and calm way. Without these key steps, setting boundaries and the potential response you receive could trigger you into past memories that will lead you to behave in a regressed way (or in a way that you would not be proud of). Both of these tools let you know when your boundaries are crossed; how much of the emotion belongs to you and your previous memories; and how much of the emotion belongs to the other party. Knowing what stuff is yours versus what is the other party's clears the path for you to work on only your concerns. For example, you recognize both that your colleagues brought up your fear of abandonment and rejection and also that their behaviour is still not acceptable. Once those fears are processed and understood with an adult mindset, you can set boundaries around how your co-workers need to communicate more transparently in the office setting.

Take Action: When we haven't grown up with emotions being validated and normalized, we often have a limited emotional vocabulary to help us process the physical sensations that we are feeling. We might be able to recognize that we feel bad, but we can't tell you what kind of "bad". While the feelings in your body might bring discomfort, this is only because of a lack of familiarity with them, after a lifetime of being told that they are negative. In effect, when we label a feeling "bad", we are placing a judgement on it and it's exceptionally difficult to process something while you are judging it. To work through our emotions, we must label it in a non-judgemental way.

The wheel of emotions, created by psychologist Robert Plutchik, is a helpful tool you can use when you need help labelling what you are feeling. Understanding what specifi-

---

cally you are feeling means that you can accurately express yourself when enforcing boundaries. Use this space to take note of what you're feeling.

_____

_____

_____

_____

_____

_____

_____

4) You Don't Know How To Set Boundaries

A lot of the difficulty in boundary setting is around the language and timing on how to set boundaries. When I was first learning boundaries, my life coach Michelle Zelli would often have to help me construct texts because I truly didn't know how to say what I wanted to say. I wasn't used to asking for what I need and want, and consistently found myself either being too lenient, and therefore unclear in what behaviour change I wanted, or too harsh, and I would include unnecessary insults in my boundaries. To find the balance between the two is definitely a learning curve and I often use Michelle's 5 Cs as a reminder when setting boundaries.

Calm: If you have processed your emotions, then you should be able to stay calm while communicating the boundary. If communicated with a raised voice, it is likely to lead to defensiveness.

Compassionate: Boundaries never have to be mean. Being compassionate to both the other party and yourself will ensure the other party doesn't feel like this is an attack, but instead a necessary conversation in order to keep your relationship healthy.

Clear: You need to be specific in what kind of behaviour change you want as a result of a boundary being set. If you don't know what outcome you want, then they won't know either. It should be crystal clear what you are asking for – and therefore even clearer when the boundary is not being respected.

Concise: Do not say more than is necessary and do not justify your feelings or why you want the behaviour change. The more you say, the more you create opportunity for the other party to nitpick at discrepancies in past events. The longer it takes to convey a boundary, the more it comes across as a discussion instead of a statement.

Consistent: The boundary does not exist if it is not reinforced when it is breached. If you set a boundary and it is broken, it is your responsibility to hold the boundary and form a consequence.

Learning how to communicate boundaries is very much like learning a new language. Throughout this book, I provide sentences and examples of boundary setting to equip you with the lexicon you need. It is when I was first given this language that light bulbs started going off in my brain. It was such unfamiliar territory that when Michelle would give me a sentence I could use, oftentimes I would respond with, "It's never occurred to me that I could say that." Other times, I would insist that I couldn't say that, and then would proceed to try it.

I've since broken down boundary setting into seven key steps in order to make sure the conversation is as productive as possible. Conveniently, the mnemonic spells out "selfish", so it's hard to forget.

Introducing the SELFISH Method

Let's use the example that your partner has gone out with their friends and they said they would be home by 10 p.m. and they aren't.

Stories:

In coaching, as I've mentioned, "stories" refer to the things we make up in our heads. In this example, the truth is your partner came home later than they said they were going to. The "story" you might be making up is that they are cheating on you, or that they don't care about you or that they never want to spend time with you. Our brain, when it has an absence of facts, will make up the rest of the story. Be aware of that. Stick to the facts. You don't know why they are late, but you know that they are. That is where you set the boundary.

Emotions:

As described in the previous chapter, make sure you have processed your own issues from your past around the current situation. In every communication, there is your stuff and there is their stuff. You need to be clear on which stuff belongs to which person and which parts you can both be accountable for. For example, in this situation, if feelings of rejection and abandonment come up, those are your feelings and you need to work through them before setting a boundary. Once you have done that, then you know your issues are about the situation in front of you.

Let go of conclusions:

People often go into difficult conversations with a foregone conclusion about what the other party thinks and, based on past experiences, how they will react. You can almost play out the whole conversation in your head before you have even had it, and a lot of people do. They rehearse these conversations and as a result enter the discussion close-minded. This leads to people being defensive in their approach because unconsciously they prepare to repeat the same pattern. Instead, enter the conversation with an open mind and allow that person the opportunity to change your mind. By being open-minded and ready to hear their response, it also means you actually listen to them as opposed to preparing your answers.

Find desired outcome:

The outcome of this conversation should be clear and should result in a behaviour change. You need to know what you are asking for. For each person, this can be different. One person could be worried about the lack of communication at night, but for another, it could be the fact that their partner has said they would do something and aren't doing it.

For another, it could be the partner's lack of concern that they are sitting at home worrying. You need to figure out which boundary of yours was crossed and what you want to go differently next time. If there was a pattern of behaviour, you can also acknowledge that.

Initiate conversation:

Choosing the right time to initiate the conversation can change the trajectory of the conversation massively. When setting a boundary in person, I tend to preface it with, "Do you have a moment to talk?" to ensure it is the right time and I have their full attention. By doing this, they are consenting to the conversation taking place and agreeing to be an active participant in it by contributing their focus. In this example, the right time might not be when your partner returns home drunk close to midnight. Instead, wait until the next morning when it will likely be less heated. If they try to talk about it at that moment, all you have to do is simply say, "Can we talk about this tomorrow? I'm tired and going to bed. I hope you had fun." Stay calm and polite – the waiting until the next morning is not a punishment or a way to prolong suspense.

Set the boundary:

State it as a fact, not a discussion. Boundaries are not a decision you make with the other party. They are not shared.

They are your boundaries that you are communicating with them. It is your decision and it is their separate decision to accept it or not. Communicating boundaries from a place of love and care for the relationship is always going to help them be accepted easily. In this example, I would simply say, "Hey! You came home later than you said you would last night. I was worried something had happened. Next time, can you text me to let me know?" It is important that the boundary is set around the behaviour and not your feelings. You cannot set a boundary asking your partner to not worry you again. You can communicate your worry, but the boundary has to focus on the behaviour. Make sure to phrase it in the positive. Ask for what you want, not what you don't want. Instead of saying "I want you to stop ignoring my texts", say "I want you to text me". If you phrase it in the negative then that is what the mind will focus on. You want the focus to be on the positive behaviour change.

Hold the boundary:

If it happens a second time, you need to hold the boundary firm. It is important that the second time you set the boundary, you include a consequence. Using the same example situation, you can say, "You said you would text me if you stayed out later. This is the second time I have brought this up and I find it disrespectful that you expect me to wait up. Next time, if you are not home when you say you are going to . . ." The consequence can vary depending on what your main issue is. If the main issue is that you are waiting up and it's your time you are concerned about, then the consequence is simply "I am going to bed without you." If the concern is that you are worried for their safety, then the consequence is that they will need to arrange to stay at a friend's house when they stay out late. If it happens again, you have to follow through with that consequence and actually lock the door when the clock hits 10pm. Then let them deal with the repercussions of their actions or the accompanying feelings they might have when they realize you were serious.

Remember that this is a new skill you are learning and the first few times, they might not take you seriously or think you will follow through because in the past you haven't. If a boundary you have set has been broken and you ignore it though, don't be surprised if they start breaking other boundaries because the message you send by not holding your boundary is that your boundaries are not important. There will be times you overcorrect and become defensive or rigid with your boundaries. Be aware of this and if you are worried about it, always say less rather than more. Be as compassionate and patient with yourself as possible. This is your first time doing something completely divergent from the pattern you have been running your entire life. It is going to take some time to unlearn your patterns and it will take some time for you to get good at setting boundaries. The first few times will be clumsy, but I promise it gets easier. Over time, you don't need to go through the steps so formally because you will automatically know what stuff is yours and when the right time to set a boundary is.

Take Action: It can be intimidating to learn something new, and putting this into action might seem daunting. To reduce the fear that you have around boundary setting, I want you to start using the phrase, "If I were able to set boundaries . . ." in every situation your brain tells you that you can't.

If I were able to set boundaries at home, I would

_____

_____

_____

_____

_____

If I were able to set boundaries at work, I would

_____

_____

_____

_____

If I were able to set boundaries with friends, I would

_____

_____

_____

If I were able to set boundaries with family, I would

If I were able to set boundaries in my love life, I would

It's amazing how starting sentences with this phrase trig-gers your brain to imagine it as if it's already a reality. Our unconscious mind doesn't know the difference between real and imagined, that's why if I tell you to imagine biting into a lemon, your body is already responding to it and likelihood is by the end of this sentence, your mouth is salivating. Your brain is doing the same thing when you imagine a reality where you can and are able to set boundaries. Our brains are very good at making things up, we just need to make sure it's making up useful things and using our imaginations to empower us by imagining a better reality.

5) Guilt After Setting Boundaries

When it comes to guilt, there is appropriate and inappropriate guilt. Appropriate guilt is necessary, because it is the way our unconscious mind tells us that we have behaved in a way that isn't aligned with our values and who we want to be. For example, this could be the guilt you feel when you turn up to work late, or you are rude to your partner because you are stressed at work. But when it comes to the guilt that follows setting boundaries, this is inappropriate guilt. Guilt is dependent on the idea you have done something wrong, and you have not done anything wrong, so you do not deserve to feel guilty. The reason why the feeling might arise anyway is because you are unlearning a lifetime of being told that standing up for yourself or saying no was selfish.

I remember the first time I cut a friend out. We had been best friends for seven years and I was right at the beginning of my journey into boundaries, so still didn't know how to articulate it and I was wracked with guilt. I listed off all the incredible things my best friend had done, including being there for me during a hospital stay, travelling cross country to see me when I was upset and organizing a surprise party when I came back to university. At one point in my life, she was a great friend, but then something changed. She had moved up north to do a master's degree, found a new friendship group and suddenly her boyfriend had become her whole world. Despite living in the same city, it would take months to organize to see each other and on the rare occasion she would call, it was only because she had a problem. The moment we were done talking about her, she would make some excuse to get off the phone, never asking about me or my life, until the next phone call when she needed something.

"I feel like I owe her. I feel guilty. She has been there for me for so many years of friendship, surely I should wait it out? She might go back to who she used to be," I said to Michelle in one of our sessions.

"How much time do you owe her?" she said in a matter-of-fact way.

"What?" I responded, confused.

"You are right, she has done all these things. How much time do you owe her? A month of friendship, a year of friendship, a decade?"

Suddenly, it seemed silly. The friend who had been there for me all those years wasn't the same person I was friends with, and then it hit me. In all that time, she had been a good friend to me, and I had been a good friend back. Now that she wasn't, I didn't owe her because I had already reciprocated in the time we were friends. I'm not saying your guilt will dissipate overnight, but realizing how much I bring to the relationships in my life made me appreciate that not everyone deserves that time and energy.

When it comes to this type of guilt, it helps to know that this feeling does not belong to you and you did nothing wrong. You can do this by either stating the words,

"I let this guilt go" or imagine it in a balloon flying away and removing the emotion from inside your body. Another way that can help is to put your hand on your heart, stroke that area in a loving and comforting way and say to yourself, "I'm proud of you, thank you for sticking up for me." Remind yourself that what you are doing is sticking up for yourself and you have done nothing wrong. Some of the guilt you might be feeling is the guilt of the emotions you have caused in the other person, but you don't need to caretake another's emotions. That is their responsibility.

You are unlearning a lifetime of society telling you that your needs are unimportant and that everyone else should come first. It is going to take time to unlearn it. I promise with each boundary you set, it becomes easier.

Take Action: A lot of guilt arises because we believe we have done the wrong thing. Providing yourself evidence for why you made the decision you did can help counter that feeling. Every time you feel guilty, get a piece of paper and write three reasons why you did the right thing:

1) I did the right thing because _____
2) I did the right thing because _____
3) I did the right thing because _____

If your guilt has extended into shame, it is likely because you have an underlying belief that you are not a good person.

Belief = Thought + evidence
Thought = Figment of your imagination

As much as it feels really bad, a feeling cannot exist without a thought preceding it, so your guilt is building evidence to support the idea that you are a bad person. To unlearn this, we need to create evidence to disprove it. If we imagine the thought as a table top, the evidence you've found in your life to support it acts like the table legs. Without the table legs, that thought, and hence the limiting belief, disappears. This is when we can start building a new table by putting evidence under a new positive thought like "I am a good person."

1) I am a good person because _____
2) I am a good person because _____
3) I am a good person because _____

6) Fear of Being Disliked

Caring what people think comes down to wanting to be liked and accepted. There are eight billion people in the world and the reality is that not everyone is going to like you. We know that logically and rationally, but the reason why it hurts so much more is because it brings up moments from our childhood when we were rejected. If this childhood wound is large enough, you turn into a people pleaser by holding onto the belief that if you change yourself enough, you can avoid that pain of being disliked – but even people pleasers can be disliked.

The fear of being disliked is often disguised by people's desire to want to be seen as "nice" or a "good person", but these words are still a preoccupation with other people's opinions. You are letting other people decide whether you are a good person by their definition, not your own. It is an obsession with others' approval, and valuing their happiness over your needs. I often say now that I am not a "nice" person, but I am a compassionate one. A nice person will do everything for you; a compassionate person will love and support you while you learn how to do things for yourself. Sometimes the most compassionate thing you can do isn't nice.

Caring what people think can come in many guises. It can come in the form of saying "yes" to something you really don't want to go to. It can be that time you said "no" when someone asked if they hurt your feelings because you didn't want them to think you were too sensitive. It can be that slight exaggeration you do at a party to seem a little more impressive or it can be going completely silent at a work event because you are intimidated and worried that you might say the wrong thing, so you say nothing at all.

Caring what people think is partially human nature. We live in a society that requires social interaction and being liked by our "in-group" in order to survive, so there is an innate aspect to it. People who don't care what people think at all and have never cared what people think are classed as psychopaths. They demonstrate no empathy and don't consider other people's thoughts at all. However, there is a distinction between those who care what others think to a healthy level and those who care so much it dictates their entire life. I'll be honest in saying that I sometimes do care about how I am perceived, of course I do, I'm human. But do I care enough to not enforce my boundary? Definitely not!

One of the beginning steps to stop caring about what people think is to remember the world doesn't revolve around us. You know when you are caught at a party alone with nobody to talk to, and you suddenly get really self-conscious that people are staring at you and thinking, "What a loser, she has no friends," so you quickly pull out your phone so that you can pretend you are doing something? We have all been there.

First of all, no one is actually looking at you as much as you think. You are the person most self-conscious about what you are doing. Everyone else is so consumed with themselves and their appearance that they often aren't thinking about you. If they do happen to catch you standing by yourself, it's probably because they are by themselves too and are relieved they aren't the only one. Yes, there is the one arsehole in every room who will look at you and be relieved they are more popular than you, but trust me, they aren't just thinking, "What a loser!" about you, they are thinking that about everyone. It's more an indication of their insecurity and a projection about the fact that they also wouldn't want to be caught alone at a social event.

The second realization is that even when people think about you, you have to remember how insignificant that thought is in the context of their day. People say judgemental things about each other all the time and then a minute later, the conversation has moved on. How long does it take to think a thought? How long does it take to think another? And you are letting those millisecond-long thoughts dictate your life? How many times have your thoughts about yourself or others been wrong? And you are going to trust some stranger's thoughts? Put it this way: they think about you for a millisecond, and perhaps say it aloud in a second or five seconds and you end up thinking about that statement for months, potentially years. How is that fair? A thought is just a figment of your imagination, so start asking yourself if your happiness is worth sacrificing for someone else's offhand thought.

The goal is not to stop caring what everyone thinks but instead to adopt these four principles:

1) People are allowed to have their opinions

Be who you are, and allow people the freedom to make a choice about you. Be unapologetic about who you are, let them have their judgements and then see if those opinions are ones that you would want in your life. Your job is not to change their thoughts, your job is to decipher if that is a person who respects and loves you.

2) I care about my opinion more than others

The only problem that comes with allowing people the freedom to make decisions about whether they like you or not is when their opinion outweighs your own. If a person doesn't like you, don't allow that to become a reason to like yourself less. You have to value your own opinion first and foremost.

3) I only care about the opinions of people I respect

You have lived with yourself your whole life and yet you are still discovering new things about yourself every day, so why are you entrusting your self-esteem to someone who knows you far less? You know yourself most intimately and therefore you are most qualified to make an assessment of yourself.

4) I will not change myself to avoid people's negative opinions of me

Part of the process of learning boundaries is being authentic to you and your needs and making sure that you are prioritizing them. If you let a person's negative opinion of you be the priority, your boundaries will never be set.

Ultimately, boundaries strengthen the good relationships in your life and destroy the ones that aren't good for you. If those are the people that end up disliking you due to your increased sense of self-worth and stronger boundaries, then it is worth it in the end.

To demonstrate that, I am going to compare two situations. Unsurprisingly, because I am a life coach, my friends often reach out to me for advice on how to respond to people, especially when boundaries are involved. My friend had been on a few dates with a guy who was quite intense and moving quickly, only to turn around after a few dates to say that it was all too much. She had sent me the text she had drafted and in the reply, her main concern was to not come across as too aggressive. The problem with this being the priority is that if you still care about how the recipient perceives you when setting your boundaries, the boundaries will automatically be weaker. I edited this aspect out of her draft and helped her send a text that would firmly close the door on a rude interaction:

"Saying how amazing I am in the same breath as 'I don't want this' is frankly rather boring. You have a lot to figure out and I need someone who can communicate clearly and all of this lack of communication has been quite the turn off. Good luck figuring things out."

She didn't end up sending it, thinking it was too brutal and that it would destroy him. Again, the concern lies with his well-being, not her own. A few months later, I found myself in a similar position. The guy I was dating was not ending it, but was disappearing for a day and then reappearing, and then disappearing for two days. The second time it happened, I sent a very similar text.

"Hey! Disappearing and then reappearing when you want sex is disrespectful and frankly a turn-off. Regardless of how casual this is, if you want a relationship with me, respect is required. If you want to end the conversation, then communicate that. If you are no longer interested, then I would prefer if you let me know, but this in-the-middle thing doesn't work for me."

When I sent the message, I had no expectation of what his reply would be. If you asked me to guess, from what I knew of him and how he had been acting so far, I expected that he would either ghost me entirely or gaslight me. I was prepared for that, and I still sent the text anyway. I believe, even if he had ghosted, his respect for me would have still gone up – he just would have been too cowardly to address the situation. That isn't what happened, though. I got a perfect apology. In my lifetime, I have rarely seen an apology that I would describe as perfect. In fact, in most relationships I have to teach people that "I'm sorry you feel that way" is not an apology, but this was exemplary. He took accountability, had a sound understanding of my feelings and offered an explanation of his intentions, as well as an "In the future, I will . . ." statement, so it did not happen again.

Of course, the difference between these two situations could have been the two sets of people involved and their level of emotional intelligence, but there is another aspect within our control: the ability to stop caring about what the other person thinks of our boundary.

Take Action: The trick with fear is that you don't need to actually get rid of it. You can just set the boundary scared. As long as the fear doesn't dictate your life, it isn't a problem. Whilst the fear of being disliked might seem large, in order to put it into context, we need to create a greater fear. By creating a greater fear, you will not only motivate yourself but it will overcompensate for the fear of being disliked or the fear of setting a boundary.

Using the example of a friend wanting to borrow money from you and you wanting to say no but are scared this will upset your friend, make your friend question your friendship or think that you are stingy. What is the greater fear? The greater fear is that without the boundary, the feeling of resentment could affect the friendship and playing out the worst case scenario, if they didn't pay you back, that could mean the end of a friendship.

The fear is that you have to have a hard conversation but the greater fear is that if you don't have the conversation, you could lose the friendship. Now create your own examples:

The Situation: _____

_____

My current fear: _____

_____

My greater fear: _____

_____

The Boundary Backlash

In the ideal scenario, when you set a boundary, the other party will respect it, change their behaviour and the conversation won't have to happen again because they will continue to respect your boundary. Unfortunately, this is not always the case. When you start loving yourself and setting boundaries, it tends to piss off the toxic people around you. One of the greatest things I've learnt in this journey of boundaries is that you don't get to control other people's reaction to you. Your only power is how you handle it. You can't stop someone treating you badly, but you can control your response and whether they are allowed in your life.

For every person who loves my honesty and appreciates my direct approach to communication, there is a person calling me aggressive, rude and arrogant. Do not measure the success of setting boundaries on how well the boundary is received. If anything, if a boundary is received badly, it's usually because they were taking advantage of your lack of boundaries. Of course, it could be because you communicated it messily, but even messy boundaries can be acknowledged with respect and a request for more clarification. When setting boundaries, it is best to remove all expectations and predictions of what their response could be. Instead of using their reaction to judge whether your boundary was acceptable or not, use it to decide if that's a person who you want in your life and whether they actually respect you.

We have to understand that the majority of people are not used to healthy communication. They have never been around it, and they don't know how to respond to it. Boundaries scare some people – they believe they mean the end of a relationship and whilst this does happen and this fear is valid, they fail to recognize that talking about the issue doesn't break the friendship – it is the inability to resolve the issue that breaks the friendship. As a result, some people will grasp at anything to convince you what just happened didn't, in an attempt to undo the situation. For other people, boundaries are a shock and the uncertainty of how to respond or react will lead them to want to protect themselves. No matter how they respond, it is important to remember two things:

- They are entitled to respond how they like
- Their response is not your responsibility

Oftentimes, when people have a negative reaction to the boundaries you set, it can be easy to start playing hypothetical situations in your head that if you had phrased your boundary another way or maybe not set it at all, you could change their reaction and their insults or hurt feelings could have been avoided. If this is the case, you are still thinking too much about the other party and not enough about how you feel.

Check in with your body. Did you feel pride or relief when you set the boundary? The likelihood is you actually felt good about your boundary and were proud of yourself before they reacted negatively. Every time you are worried about their reactions, come back to yourself. Anytime I have a client who starts worrying how the other person feels, I respond with, "What about you?" I want you to get in the habit of asking yourself the same thing. Ask yourself "What about me?" What do I want? What do I need? What do I feel? Become more selfish and think about yourself. Part of this process is starting to prioritize your needs over another person's feelings. Their feelings are their responsibility and if they do the emotional work that is required, they will heal from that.

In one of the situations where I set boundaries, I was in a WhatsApp group chat with two of my friends and for context, they were best friends with each other. I was good friends with them both and when we hung out, it would often be the three of us together, but the level of friendship between me and them was unmatched to the level of friendship they had between themselves, and it worked well – until it didn't. The night that we got into an argument, we were having a pedantic conversation about perfectionism. I was saying that I believe that perfectionism is an excuse to hide fear, namely the fear of rejection, and one of my friends was disagreeing with me. We had butted heads a few times in the last few months and one of the biggest issues I had is that she was incapable of disagreeing without getting personal. I had witnessed it happening a number of times with other friends, but it hadn't happened with me directly. This was the first time it was happening with me and it is a strong boundary of mine. There is no need to ever insult a person in an argument. Arguments should be about resolving the disagreement, not about winning or losing or about hurting the other party the most. The conversation escalated and ended with a bunch of passive-aggressive comments and insults, at which point I simply replied, "Ouch. I am going to take some space from this conversation." The conversation didn't stop, but I stopped replying. I attempted to re-enter the conversation calmly a few hours later and that's when I was met with more insults and decided to end the friendship and I communicated that.

Oftentimes, it isn't the actual incident that makes me decide I don't want to be in the relationship but actually how the confrontation is dealt with. The original issue doesn't break the friendship, it's the words thrown during the fight that breaks the friendship. Now when I set a boundary, and it isn't respected, I see it as a clear warning sign. In this situation though, there was a third person in the mix and while I told the third person not to involve herself in the conversation, she wanted to fix this friendship more than I wanted to. Even though it wasn't her situation, she was allowed to have her feelings about two friends falling out and because I was still friends with her, I agreed to give her a call and listen. It was in the call that she told me the way I live my life is too unforgiving and that I can't just cut people out when they fuck up once. She also made a comment that I would never find a boyfriend if I keep acting this way. Both of these comments were manipulation. They were using her knowledge as a close friend to hit me where it hurts both in terms of the fact that I had lost a number of friends in the last year and the fact that I had started wanting a relationship for the first time in many years. At this point, I had already had two years of experience with boundaries, so I could see it as manipulation and I didn't take it personally. But this situation also required some boundaries being set because I don't tolerate manipulation. After the phone call, I sent the following text:

> Hey! I know I assured you that we wouldn't fall out over this but I don't feel good about the friendship any more and the way this conversation has escalated is not something I could have foreseen. I know from our phone call that you have the perception that I cut people out over one incident, but this is far from the case. Every friendship I have lost this year has been a build-up and a pattern and I would lose them all again for the person I am becoming. This was not one incident and you know that. I also want to bring up the fact that you mentioned on the phone that "I'm never going to find a boyfriend if I keep acting like this." I was shocked when you said this because you are a feminist and this is a very archaic statement and is inappropriate, especially as we were not talking about boyfriends or my love life. I hope you both have a good time tomorrow! Xx

If you are unsure in the boundaries you set, then that's when you open a gap for others to manipulate you. Manipulation is seen as quite an extreme term but at its simplest definition, it is trying to influence someone to change their behaviour. In this case, she was trying to influence me to heal the friendship I had decided to end. If you are certain in how you deserve to be treated, sentences like the one about me being single stick out. It stuck out in the conversation when she said it. It took me off guard enough that I didn't know how to react to it over the phone but as soon as I hung up, it left a heavy feeling in my chest. With experience, you will start to recognize these statements as manipulation and your first instinct will be to say, "Do not speak to me like that" instead of "Are they right?" She apologized, and to this day we are still friends. She may still think I am too unforgiving and that is her right. I have never checked or tried to fix her perception of who I am because I am happy with who I am and the decisions I have made.

One of the fundamental steps of getting over this obstacle is realizing that people are allowed to have their opinions. She can think I'm unforgiving. She is allowed to think I cut people out too quickly and that I have cut out too many people out of my life. She is allowed to have all those opinions and I am not going to try to change them because her opinion of me is not within my control, nor should it be. Allow people to have their opinions. Allow them to believe that the decisions you make are wrong. Allow them to think that your demands are too high and that you have too many needs. Their opinion of you is none of your business. If you go out of your way to try to avoid opinions, you will never live your life to your full potential.

In other situations, the backlash that you receive from setting a boundary can result in gaslighting. People with weak boundaries tend to attract people who take advantage of those boundaries so when you start standing up for yourself, this will become inconvenient to them and therefore they will use whatever tactic they can to get you to weaken your boundary. Sometimes, this is simply insults like the example I gave above. Common words that are thrown around are: mean, bully, harsh and unforgiving. In the worst cases, gaslighting will be involved. This could be convincing you that you are "crazy", that their emotions are your fault, or distorting your memories by insisting the situation that just took place never happened. How do you know if you are being gaslit? You will feel confused. You will be confused about how you think, what you feel and whether your memories are accurate.

Gaslighting, by definition, is the action of manipulating someone by psychological means into accepting a false depiction of reality or doubting their own sanity. The word comes from the 1938 play *Gaslight* by Patrick Hamilton – made famous by the subsequent Oscar-winning 1944 film of the same title – in which a man manipulates his wife into believing that she is going insane. The title, from which the concept takes its name, is a reference to the husband's insistence that the woman is imagining the gas lights brightening and dimming, when in reality he is dimming the gas lights himself.

A gaslighter will try to attempt to warp your memories or undermine your feelings. They could pretend they didn't say what they said or accuse you of being "too sensitive" or "too needy". In Harriet Lerner's book *Why Won't You Apologize?*, she states, "Questioning ourselves for being oversensitive is a common way that women in particular disqualify our legitimate anger and hurt." I would extend that and say that questioning how sensitive or needy you are not only disqualifies your emotions, but it also undermines the boundary you set. Your emotions are legitimate and the people who accuse you of being too sensitive are often not being sensitive enough. In terms of being called "too needy", I would alter that to "I am too needy *for you*," meaning that I have needs you cannot satisfy and therefore this does not work. What it does not mean is that I ignore my needs in order to keep you in my life.

The word "needy" is also a word that is predominantly used to label women and I believe this idea is fuelled by the media. Women who have needs are shown as annoying, naggy and unattractive and the likeable attractive women are always the ones who have no expectations of others and are willing to go along with anything. It is conveyed in multiple different archetypes from the naggy girlfriend to the boss who is a bitch to conversely, the "chill girl who can hang with the boys" and the "manic pixie dream girl" who is so floaty and carefree that everyone loves her. None of these archetypes have needs or insist on being treated better, but exist to make the male characters look better. Societally, when women speak up for themselves, they are seen as difficult but if a man said the same thing, it would be perceived as him having "standards". Therefore, to counter this, we need to start from a place of believing that our emotions and needs are valid and legitimate. Stop comparing yourself to other people and seeing it as a competition as to who can be the most low maintenance. You are allowed to ask for more; you are allowed to expect more. If we continue to question how we feel and whether we are allowed to feel that way, we doubt ourselves and are unsure about what we are doing. When we don't know what to do, we look to others to tell us what to do. So when you first set boundaries, and their response is a gaslighting one, we take that as an indication that what we have done was wrong. But it wasn't! All that is happening is that you are looking for approval in a place where you are not going to get any. You have wired your brain, and designed your life, to constantly seek praise because you have felt uncertain in your own decisions. This is the chance to rewire that programming.

The intention of gaslighting is for the person to get you to trust them more than your own instinct, emotions and memory. They want you to doubt yourself, and that is why gaslighting is often used within boundary setting. If you have set firm lines in the sand, manipulators are unable to take advantage of and control you in the same way. This frustrates and often angers them because they lose their power over you. If you are highly empathetic, this is easily overlooked. Empathetic people tend to see the good in people, and while this is often romanticized in our society as a positive trait, it means they don't clock red flags and warning signs that they should have noticed in the beginning. They see only the good, as opposed to seeing the reality.

The most important thing to remember is that if a person respects you, they will respect your boundary even if it is inconvenient for them. If a person responds in anger or with gaslighting, then that boundary was needed more than ever, because it demonstrates that they were taking advantage of you. Every time you are called mean, selfish or a bully, you are doing it right. You are not a nice person for allowing someone to take advantage of you and you are not mean for not allowing them to. The silver lining is that once you get used to setting boundaries, these people will automatically leave your life. It isn't fun for them when you aren't of service to them or they can't manipulate you to do what they want. They do not have to agree with your boundary in order for you to enforce it.

If you do not feel safe enforcing a boundary

It is important to make an exception if you do not feel safe in setting a boundary. Fear and guilt is normal, but if your safety is in danger and the person you are setting a boundary with is capable of retaliating with physical violence or emotional abuse, then it might be safer to emotionally disconnect and detach. In these cases, if possible, please get yourself out of the situation. Of course, there are situations where this is not possible. These include when you are under the age of 18 and the person crossing your boundaries is a parent. This is the same as if you are older than 18 but still financially dependent on your parents.

Similarly, I have had people tell me stories about how setting boundaries would lead to the abuser cutting off their contact to someone they love. An example of this was a father who didn't have primary custody and whose ex-wife would be able to cut off his contact with his son. In these sorts of situations, you may choose to not enforce boundaries in order to keep the other person in your life – but if that is your choice, make it a conscious decision. See it as a transactional relationship so that when your ex-partner crosses your boundaries, in your mind you can tell yourself that you are doing this for your child. Remove the idea that you will be able to change the situation and get rid of the hope that your ex will change. This unrealistic expectation is what causes a lot of the pain. You are making the best of a bad situation and although at this time the toxic dynamic is unavoidable, you are able to control your emotional attachment to the situation. When you disconnect emotionally, you are able to foster a sense of numbness when communicating with your ex and that removes their power to rattle you emotionally.

Take Action: Gaslighters tend to target people whom they know they can take advantage of. The impact of gaslighting can make you feel weak. To remind yourself that there is a strong version of you inside, here is a coaching exercise that I did during my training. We were asked to "act as if" we were something we weren't. I want you to act as if you are really good at setting boundaries and that you have done it for years. It is second nature to you. Close your eyes and imagine it as vividly as you can until you feel that strength in your body. Then I want you to recall a time when you felt most powerful and go into that memory. Sit how you were sitting, breathe how you were breathing. Move to the strongest part of yourself and ask yourself how you would react in the same situation now. You are able to recall that part of you because it exists inside you. The next time you feel you are being gaslit, remind yourself to respond from the most empowered part of you.

Common Responses To Boundaries

The common responses to boundaries that include gaslighting are so predictable that they become boring. Below, I have suggested replies you can use when someone is gaslighting you. While none of these replies can make a person stop gaslighting you, it may provide you with some power to feel like you are equipped with responses. If you use these responses, please remember not to feed into the idea that if you say the right thing, you can avoid fights. This is both protective behaviour and inaccurate, because communication requires both parties. Your response cannot change the person's desire to gaslight you, but these responses might help you not internalize their perception of you. Learning that their responses are predictable and identifying them as a pattern can help diminish the pain the words cause.

They say: "You are crazy"

You can say:

"Responding in a way that you would not respond does not make me crazy."

This response acknowledges that they might not understand your reaction and also reaffirms that you stand by your boundary. It also demonstrates that their perception of you being crazy has not been internalized by you.

"Stop gaslighting me"

Calling out gaslighting when it occurs takes away the power it has over you. This is a demand about how you deserve to be treated. Even if the other party disagrees or doesn't understand what gaslighting is, it allows you to label it as such.

"You are allowed to think that and I am still asking for what I am asking for."

When this is said in response to a boundary, it is being said to make you question yourself and undermine your boundary in the hopes that you are concerned about their perception of you. This sentence reinforces that you still want your needs met, no matter how crazy the other person thinks they are.

They say: "You are making a big deal out of nothing."
Similar alternative: "You are overreacting."

You can say:

"It might not be a big deal to you, but it is to me, and if you care about me, then you should care about what matters to me."

This is an attempt to try to diminish the importance of a subject that matters to you and this response reclaims its importance because it states that it doesn't need to be important to both parties in order for it to be of importance.

"If you don't understand my feelings, then ask – but do not diminish my feelings."

The question they should be asking, instead of gaslighting, is "Why has this created such a big reaction?" This alternative phrasing of the question is not borne from defensiveness, so it gives you the opportunity to explain the reasoning behind the feelings.

"Are you aware of how that makes me feel?"

This is a "take a breath and a step back" response. Since their statement came out of defensiveness, this is a non-confrontational way of not reacting. It is offering them a detour in the conversation, which they can either take or ignore and plow on with their defensiveness.

They say: "You are being too sensitive."

Similar alternatives: "You are irrational," "You are so thin-skinned."

You can say:

"Have you considered that you aren't being sensitive enough?"

"Have you considered" is a good softener that can be added to any other statement. This suggestion that they are not being sensitive enough removes the objectivity of their statement that they are the person who decides how much sensitivity is appropriate.

"Yes, and I wish you would respect my sensitivity to this topic."

"Yes, and" is a good communication tool that again can be used in all responses. They have framed sensitivity as an insult in this communication and by agreeing with their statement, it reframes it as neither an insult nor a compliment but a fact.

"Am I?"

This again is another response that allows them to take a step back and re-evaluate their behaviour and offers them an opportunity to retract their accusation. The key to using this statement is to state it as powerfully as you can. Do not state it as if you are questioning your own sensitivity.

They say: "You are so emotional."

You can say:

"Yes, I am an emotional person. All humans are emotional."

This prevents them from using this statement as a way to derail the conversation into an argument about whether or not you are emotional. The longer you argue about your emotions, the less the conversation is about the actual content of the disagreement.

"I am glad you have noticed how your words affect others."

The underlying message in their initial statement is that being emotional is a bad thing. If you believe that emotions are not a bad thing and not something to be wielded against each other, then it is not an insult. This twists it around and takes it from an accusation they made to simply an observation.

"Emotion and rationale are not mutually exclusive."

The accusation of being emotional comes with the assumption that you can't "think straight" or that you aren't responding or acting appropriately because you are "in your emotions". They can exist together and this statement confirms your certainty of that.

They say: "It's just a joke!"

Similar alternatives: "You have no sense of humour," "Do you have to take everything so seriously?"

<u>You can say:</u>

"Saying something passive-aggressive and passing it off as a joke doesn't make it a joke."

When someone says it's a joke, both parties tend to know it isn't. What has actually happened is they have said something cutting and do not want to face the repercussions of it. This comment dismisses that hurt so that you can't have your reaction – and if you do have a reaction, then you don't have a sense of humour. Describing it as what it is, passive aggression, is key because it allows you to not internalize it.

"Jokes that hurt others aren't funny."

This is an alternative if you think that the first sentence is going to derail the conversation into a discussion about what qualifies as a joke and what doesn't. Societally, the idea of what is funny has shifted dramatically since the rise in social consciousness, meaning that people often think that humour is not allowed and no one has a sense of humour anymore. Of course, this is not true; people have a sense of humour, but a joke is not funny if it comes at the expense of a marginalized group. This is the same on the personal level. If the humour is coming at the cost of you, then it's not funny.

"Is there something you want to say to me?"

This question addresses the fact that they have said something hurtful and are now using a cop-out to deflect. It asks the person to stand by what they said and sometimes I would add that in: "If you have something to say to me, then say it and stand by your words."

They say: "It's free speech, I can say what I want."

You can say:

"Yes, and because I have free will, I don't have to listen to it."

Free speech is a phrase that gets used often as a push back against people becoming more socially conscious. If they want to emphasize their freedom, then you can emphasize your own. You never have to stay in a conversation that makes you uncomfortable. In the best situation, you would say you are leaving the conversation and explain why. In situations where this is not appropriate, say you are going to get a drink or going to the bathroom.

"You are allowed free speech and I am allowed my reaction."

This is not a conversation about what can be said, but more so about what *should* be said. If you knew your words were hurting other people and you intentionally chose to keep saying those words, then that is where the issue lies. There may be free speech but there are also consequences to free speech, whether that be your reaction or the impact of that free speech on your relationship. Words have impact and once spoken, they are rarely forgotten. Someone who is emotionally intelligent would take responsibility for the words that come out of their mouth.

"I'm not saying you can't say it. I'm saying that you can't say it to me."

This can be used in situations where you are asking someone not to have specific conversations with you about something or someone. It could be that you want to stop gossiping and so are asking your friend to talk to the person they have an issue with, or it could be that your friend who is still friends with your ex can't stop talking about them, and you need them to stop so that you can heal from the breakup.

They say: "I never said/did that."

<u>You can say:</u>

"I am not debating whether it happened or not."

The intention of this tactic is for you to doubt your memories. Stating this sentence or similar reinstates that you are not going to doubt yourself. Twisting your memories is a form of gaslighting, and it's how a lot of victims of gaslighting end up feeling like they are going crazy because they no longer trust their version of events.

"If we are going to continue this conversation, I am going to need you to be honest."

This homes in on the fact that conversations should be focused on a resolution. If one party is denying that an event took place, then the purpose of the conversation won't be fulfilled. This essentially states that it is their choice whether this conversation continues, and for you to be a part of it, you need them to be honest.

"I am going to step away from this conversation. Come back to me when you are willing to take accountability for your actions/words."

Some people need time and space in order to lower their defences and not be speaking from a place of protection and ego. This is the next step I would use if they continue to lie. Conversations where you end up in a circle of debating what happened and what didn't are not productive, and can actually add more problems that you will need to resolve.

They say: "You are mean."

<u>You can say:</u>

"You are allowed to think that."

Their perception of you and their perception of the fact that you are mean is simply that, a perception. Allowing them to have that belief while knowing it's not accurate releases you from needing to control what they think of you. It takes away the emotional potency of the word when you just accept that is their point of view.

"If that's what I need to be in order for you to respect me, then so be it."

The word "mean" is often thrown around when someone is losing their ability to control you. They are so used to you being easily taken advantage of and being "too nice" that anything that is neutral, like setting boundaries, is perceived as mean.

"Is standing up for myself the same as being mean?"

This throws it back into their court and forces them to reflect on their assumptions. They have equated you knowing your self-worth to being mean and this response puts them in a position where they have to explain the distinction. Asking a question when someone makes a statement like this also dissipates the situation. You can continue to do this, so if they respond with, "No, but you are being really smug about it," then you can reply, "Which sentence came across as smug?" This helps them build a greater understanding of what they've said, and in most cases, it unravels their argument because they are unable to substantiate their claims that you are mean.

They say: "You are such a bully."

You can say:

"It's a shame you feel that way."
This comment, like many of the others, is designed to provoke a reaction. The hope is that you will feel attacked and then the conversation will become about your need to defend yourself from accusations. Accepting that you can't control what they think of you changes the dynamic because they are accustomed to you reacting, and this low-investment answer changes the trajectory of the conversation. It may even catch them off guard by not providing the reaction they were expecting.

"Insulting me is not going to make me change my mind."
When setting a boundary, words like "bully" are often thrown around to make you question whether you have been too harsh in your boundary. Reinforcing that boundary and maintaining it no matter what comments they make or how hurtful their words are is imperative to the process. Demonstrate that your decision was made to keep your boundary from becoming a debate. It is not a discussion – it is a decision that you have already made.

"Bullies hurt others. I am just refusing to let you continue to hurt me."

What better way for them to derail the conversation than to call you out for exactly what they are doing? It puts you in a double bind and prevents you from accusing them of the same thing. Make the distinction between your behaviour and their own, focusing on the idea that you doing what is best for you is different to doing something with the intention of affecting someone else.

Take Action: With this knowledge, have a look back at times in your life when you attempted to set a boundary and were met with one of these responses. Were you actually in the right? What would you say to them now, with this new information that you have? Writing out what you would have done differently can help you let go of past resentments because it reaffirms the knowledge that you would know what to say now.

_____

_____

_____

_____

_____

_____

_____

_____

THE JOY OF BEING SELFISH

CHAPTER 3:

THE STAGES OF BOUNDARY SETTING

No: What Do You Actually Want?

Just because the phone is ringing doesn't mean you have to pick up. Just because someone wants you doesn't mean they get to have you. Just because someone needs you for something doesn't mean you have to drop your own needs. It's time to stop being dictated by the needs and wants of the world around you and start asking yourself what *you* actually want.

People with good boundaries say what they mean and they mean what they say. In that sense, "no" is a hugely symbolic word, and our inability to use it when we want to is a sign of lack of boundaries. It is the word we use to make choices and decisions for our life. If we are unable to use it effectively, our lives are decided by others and we become a victim to our own life. When we don't have boundaries, we say yes when we mean no, and as a result we rarely get a chance to say yes to the things we want to do. This is why learning how to say no also gives our yes more power. Reintroducing no into your vocabulary puts you back in charge of making decisions for yourself.

The first time I remember saying the word "no", I was 15 years old. My sister, who is 12 years older than me, had taken me out for lunch and my food had arrived cold. Some may say I was simply being British, but I refused to tell the waiter, staying silent even when he came over and asked if I was enjoying the food. My sister then said, "No, my sister isn't happy," and waited for me to finish the complaint. There were a number of reasons why I didn't say no. In my shy, teenage-girl head, I didn't want to upset the waiter. I didn't want to be annoying. I didn't want to be difficult. I didn't want to make him uncomfortable and I didn't want to come across as demanding. While this conversation with a complete stranger about food seems trivial, the thoughts that came into my mind were the exact same feeling as if I was setting a more vital boundary with someone I cared about. How you act in minor situations is often a predictor of how you will act in significant ones. So while it might seem silly, if you can say no to a waiter when they ask if you are happy with your food, it can give you the confidence and strength to say no when more is at stake.

As soon as the waiter left, in typical sisterly fashion, I told my sister how embarrassing she was and how unnecessary all of that was, but that experience would actually end up being a seminal lesson in asking for what I need. This is exactly where it begins, in everyday interactions. How many times have you told a hairdresser you were happy when you weren't? How many times have you replied to

"Are you OK?" with a yes, when you really wanted to say no? Being able to use the word "no" is a vital step and the first introduction to boundaries.

Knowing what you want might seem like a big ask if you are someone who doesn't understand themselves well. Especially in the beginning stages of boundaries, it can feel like an impossible task. What I have found is that even when you don't know what you want, most people are able to tell you what they *don't* want. I often give this advice in the context of teenagers leaving school and university and choosing a career. They might not know what they want to do, but if you ask them what they definitely don't want to do, they will have a list. You start with that. The list of "do not"s provides valuable information and those are your no's when it comes to boundary setting.

When talking about saying no, the most common question is, "But how do I do it?" When people ask this, they aren't actually asking how to make the word "no" come out of their mouth, but actually how to do it without discomfort. There is no solution to this. All personal growth is uncomfortable, and if you aren't willing to do the work of going through that discomfort, you can continue to choose the life you are currently living. However, then you are not allowed to keep complaining that no one respects your boundaries if you are unable to set them. You picked up this book because you wanted change, and that change is not going to happen by simply reading the words in this book. You need to put it into action. How you start saying no is by actually saying that word for the first time, facing that discomfort and realizing it is not as bad as the story you've created in your head. You then proceed to do it over and over until it becomes normal for you to say no when you mean no and only say yes when you want to say yes.

To know when you need to say no, you need to know firmly what you want. You have spent so long not listening to your needs and desires that this part of your internal voice might be hard to locate. Check in with your body before making a decision. You will know when you should have said no when it doesn't feel good to say yes. You will feel resentment or anger, or even dread, at agreeing to do something you don't want to do. If you ask yourself why you said the opposite of what you intended, the response will always be about the other person.

"Because he needed help."
"Because they will hate me if I don't."
"Because she gets angry when I say no."

In more complicated decisions, where your inner voice has been confused with other people's needs and desires, it is useful to look back on the previous values exercise (see page 50) and remind yourself of what's important to you. Now that you are aware of what you need for fulfilment in each area of life, decisions are easier. Let's say your top values in your career are money, appreciation and respect, and your boss asks if you would like to switch departments. You can now ask yourself if that role change would lead to an increase in money, appreciation or respect, and make a choice based on that assessment.

The main obstacle to saying no is worrying about being disliked, so the true lesson of no is prioritizing what you need over what someone else thinks. You can't actually know what someone thinks and you also can't know how someone is going to react, so the solution is to stop thinking about the other person at all. Stay grounded in your own body and whenever thoughts stray to the other person, return to that habit of asking yourself, "What about me? What do I want?"

What you want becomes a lot clearer when you keep the focus on yourself. I realized this the first time I said no to a best friend. I did it because it was part of my "Year of No", but until this point I prided myself on being an extraordinary friend. In fact, on my twenty-first birthday, my best friends got up and shared moments of this in action – I had jumped on a train with an hour's notice because they were sad, I would turn up at their door with hot chocolate and would bend over backwards to make everyone else happy. While this sounds lovely and admirable, if I was honest with myself, all of these behaviours came from an insecure part of me that didn't believe I was good enough. I truly believed the only reason people were friends with me was because I was reliable, and it's always handy to have a friend who will be there no matter what. The part that is missed out is how often being there for everyone else came at the expense of my own life. Ironically, playing this reliable role confirmed my insecurity and created a belief that I was unimportant because everyone else came first.

So I said no to my best friend when she asked for something I did not want to give. And then I was racked with guilt. I took this to my life coach Michelle and she responded simply, "It's more self-centred that you think she can't survive without you, and you are underestimating her when you think she isn't going to be alright without you." She was right. Sometimes we exaggerate our own importance in someone else's life and as a result, accidentally undermine the competence of the people around us.

How often have you felt guilty for turning down a party invitation? The underlying assumption is that they wouldn't be having as much fun without you or that they would be so sad without your presence that they wouldn't be able to enjoy the rest of the party. How about when you say "no" to hanging out with your boyfriend? You make the assumption that he would be sad because he wouldn't have other plans. We make up a lot of stories about how someone else is going to feel about your no, but it is not based on reality. In the beginning, you might find it useful to give yourself some time before you give your knee-jerk assent, and if you need a baby step before you say no, then create some time with these options:

"Let me get back to you."
"Can you give me some time to think about it?"

"I am not sure yet, but I will let you know by Friday." (Give a specific time when possible and make sure you DO let them know and don't just use this as an excuse to get them to drop it. Not following up means you are building a relationship on dishonesty.)

Give yourself some distance to actually consider what you want. You are allowed to take your time and not give an instant reply. If you consider it and then decide not to go, here are a few ways to return to the conversation:

"Hey! I thought about it and it's a no from me."
"Just following up from last week – unfortunately, I can't make it work."

Usually I will end it with "Have fun though!" or "Good luck with your event!" but what I rarely do is provide a reason. People are accustomed to justifying their choices, and this is why, when I made that New Year's resolution to say no, I also added a clause that I couldn't justify it. "No" can be a really empowering word, but you diminish that power when you spend time justifying it. Doing so merely demonstrates your own discomfort and still places too much of an emphasis on the other party and your need for their approval. The reason why I rarely give a reason is because it gives people the opportunity to poke holes in your explanation. If you said you didn't want to go to a house party because you had too much work, the other party responds as if this is a problem to be fixed ("Well, how about if you work now? You'll be done before the party has even started.") If you don't provide a reason or, if pushed, you respond with, "Because I said so" or "Because I don't want to," there is nothing to refute. Of course, in some situations, a reason may be needed, but for the most part, it's not. You do not need to justify your no and most of all, other people don't have to like or agree with your no, in the same way that other people don't need to understand your boundaries.

Take Action: In life coaching, there is a phrase we use: "Stop should-ing yourself." The word "should" is a tool of self-abuse. We use it to do things we don't want to do but would feel bad saying no to. It is laced in shame; instead of providing options, it traps us in negative emotions. Whenever you feel the temptation to say the words "I should," replace them with "I want to." Let's use some examples:

"I should go to that party tonight." → "I want to go to that party tonight."

"I should spend time with my husband." → "I want to spend time with my husband."

Let's say you actually don't want to spend time with your husband, and that doesn't feel true when you say it. Well, then the exercise has served its purpose. This task is all about deciphering what you actually want and what society tells you that you want. If you don't want it, then stop guilting yourself and be true to your actual desires.

Ouch: Learning to Express Yourself When Your Boundaries Are Crossed

It is crucial to recognize when your boundaries have been crossed. Some of the time this will be obvious because you can hear your inner voice telling you that you want to do one thing and you choose another to please the people around you, but sometimes it is not as obvious. In these situations, the biggest indicator is resentment or anger. Other indications could be the feeling of helplessness or powerlessness, as well as frustration or confusion. These feelings don't always arise in the moment, especially if you have normalized boundary violations as a part of everyday life. Have you ever left a conversation and then felt bad about something that was said? That was a boundary violation. Once you can identify it as a boundary violation, you can do something about it.

The problem is people with no boundaries are so accustomed to questioning their feelings and doubting whether their anger or annoyance is valid, it's easier to keep to their old habit of "sweeping it under the carpet" or "not rocking the boat". This idea of keeping the peace is false because in reality, it means disturbing your own inner peace. When has there been a time this has worked without you feeling internal resentment or without it affecting your behaviour around the person? When we are unsure of whether we are allowed to feel that way, we often ask someone else. But this is pointless – two humans can feel differently about the same issue, so who is to say the other person is right and you are not? When something is said that makes you feel bad, all you need to know is that you are allowed to feel that way.

We start to combat this by validating that how you feel is real and important. This might sound like common sense, but it's not. I know that because every day I am asked questions that start with, "Is it normal that . . .?" or "Is it weird if . . .?" or "Is it OK . . .?" As soon as you go to an external person to decide what is acceptable, you are giving away your power. All emotions are normal. All emotions are healthy and you are allowed to feel how you feel. There are no exceptions to that rule. Once you start giving yourself permission to have your feelings, it will become easier to notice when someone's words or actions have made you feel bad. You won't always notice in the moment, especially at the beginning, but luckily, there is no statute of limitations on boundary setting.

Once we know how we feel and we let ourselves feel it, we can decide to express ourselves and set a boundary. This is where a second level of doubt comes in. Is my boundary ridiculous? Am I being unreasonable? If the boundary is what you want, then it is the correct one for you. No two people will have the same boundaries. Boundaries are about protecting you, so only you can say if they are appropriate or not. It is not anyone else's right to tell you that your boundary is wrong, even if they don't agree with it.

Learning the language around, and how to articulate, your boundaries will take practice, but it all starts with expressing yourself after the initial boundary violation. When we go about changing our lives, we can often bounce from one extreme to another. We create this false choice between saying nothing at all or being really combative, when actually there is a middle ground that I discovered with the word "ouch".

The first time I heard the word "ouch" in the context of boundaries was actually when I crossed someone else's boundary – my life coach, Michelle's. She was trying to help me resolve an issue and told me she had some time later on in the day if I needed an emergency session. In my defensive state, I pushed the offer away. I used to be awful at asking for help and while I have improved dramatically since then, five years ago, I was still operating out of my defence mechanism and shoving people away when they were trying to help. She responded simply with one line, "Ouch. I will keep the 4 p.m. slot open for you." There was something about the word "ouch" that made me realize what I had done. In a strange way, it made me accountable for how I made others feel more than any word, phrase or lecture had. One small word made me aware of my own defences and allowed me to realize that my words have impact. That is why I believe in its power now – because I know how effectively it worked on me.

The best thing with this word is it can be used as your beginner's tool. If boundaries are feeling daunting and overwhelming, make yourself the promise to at least express when your boundaries are crossed, even if you aren't ready to do anything about them yet. I personally think "ouch" is the most powerful, but if it doesn't feel very you, here are a few other alternatives:

- "That's not a very nice thing to say."
- "That hurts."
- "Can you say that again?"
- "Did you mean that to sound as offensive as it was?"
- "Wow." (not to be used with a sarcastic tone, but with genuine hurt)

The trick with all of these is to hold your power by letting the silence exist. Silence in conversations makes people uncomfortable and while you might be feeling some of that discomfort, if you own it, you will see that the discomfort doesn't belong to you, it belongs to the other party. Most people won't have the audacity to repeat a rude sentiment or behaviour, but if they do, then not only have you given them an opportunity to apologize, but you've also bought yourself some time to prepare yourself to set the boundary.

You might find saying something as simple as "ouch" or "That hurts" feels like a step towards building your self-esteem, because by vocalizing something, anything, you have declared that your feelings matter and are important. By defending yourself, you are teaching yourself that you are worth protecting. We protect things of value, so you are showing yourself that you are valuable.

Take Action: Boundaries were a huge step in me learning about the importance of language and how we use it. Having pre-prepared phrases like "Ouch!" or "Did you mean that to sound as offensive as it was?" helped me gain the confidence to articulate other boundaries in my life and it also made me more conscious of the language I use with myself. The examples below show the different ways in which you can use language to change your mindset.

"Yet"

How many times do you tell yourself you can't do something? Switch "I can't stand up for myself" to "I can't stand up for myself yet." Embedded in this little word is the assumption that you will get there one day, and that helps in being able to achieve it.

Limiting Belief: I can't set boundaries
New Belief: I can't set boundaries yet

Limiting Belief: _____
_____
New Belief: _____
_____

"Always/never"

This is one that we all need to stop using with ourselves and each other. Mid-argument, it is so tempting to say, "You never listen to me!" as opposed to "You are not listening to me." These generalizations keep us stuck, even if you are just using them with yourself. If you are telling yourself, "I am always such a pushover," what hope do you have of changing that behaviour? Another key part is remembering that you are not your behaviour; there is a difference between "I am being a pushover" and "I am a pushover." We are all capable of being a pushover, but that doesn't mean we claim that label and add it to our identity and live in that space.

Limiting Language: You never unload the dishwasher!
Empowered Language: You have not unloaded the dishwasher this week.

Limiting Language: _____

_____

Empowered Language: _____

_____

"Kiddo"
We can't control the mean thoughts inside our head that like to pipe up when we dare to venture outside of our comfort zone. Though it's impossible to jump in front of a thought before it exists, what you can do is add softeners. If your brain starts screaming at you, "You are so useless, you can't even set boundaries!", notice the shift in energy if you just add the word "kiddo" at the end. Don't like kiddo? Try darling or sweetheart or a pet name that you would use with someone you love. "You are so useless, darling" suddenly doesn't have the kick

it had before and doesn't carry the same emotional punch to the gut. Use it enough times and you will be surprised how the mean thoughts gain less traction.

Your own list of pet names:

_____

_____

_____

_____

"What I'm telling myself"
This phrase is really powerful in acknowledging that your thoughts are not always accurate. You can use this both internally and in conversations with other people. Saying, "I am telling myself that she doesn't love me" acknowledges that your perception is not the reality. Similarly, in a conversation with another person, rather than accusing them of not loving you, you could say, "When you behave that way, I tell myself that you don't love me." It gives people the chance to respond without getting defensive because you are owning your own thoughts and also giving them the benefit of the doubt by creating room for the fact that how you see things isn't the only way it can be perceived.

What I'm Telling Myself: My colleague took my work and passed it off as his own. What I'm telling myself is that he saw my work, knew it was good but was too lazy to come up with his own idea so stole mine and because our boss likes him more than me, she will only acknowledge him and praise him. What I'm telling myself is that my work never gets any notice and everyone in this office hates me anyway.

The Facts: My colleague and I submitted similar pieces of work. I do not know if his idea was his own or taken from my work. I feel underappreciated at work. I will ask him for clarity.

What I'm Telling Myself:

_____

_____

_____

_____

_____

The Facts:

_____

_____

_____

_____

_____

"What I'm making up"

Just as with the last phrase, when you are in an emotional conversation, it is imperative to recognize the difference between facts and the blanks you are filling in. Whether it's your internal voice or your external one, saying, "When you interrupt me when I am speaking, I am making up that you think I am stupid" acknowledges that you are assigning meanings to things that haven't been said. This means the other party can take accountability for their part of it, and even in your head, you can differentiate between how you feel and what happened, which gives you more power.

What I'm Making Up: When my brother makes comments about how I let my kids have iPads, what I'm making up is that he is judging my parenting and calling me a bad mother.

The Facts: My brother doesn't let his kids have iPads. I let my kids have iPads. Whether my kids have iPads is not his decision. I feel judged. I need to ask him to stop commenting on my parenting choices.

What I'm Making Up:

_____

_____

_____

_____

_____

The Facts:

_____

_____

_____

_____

_____

I Wish I Could Come but I Don't Want to: Declining Invitations

We have been socialized to think that telling "white lies" is kinder than to tell someone that you don't want to come. How many times have you pretended you were sick or that you had a "family emergency"? It's so commonplace that when we hear these excuses being used on us, even we don't believe them, so what's the harm? The harm is that we break our own self-trust. If we can't trust the words we say to other people, then how are we meant to trust the words we say to ourselves? We need to build a foundation of trust in the promises we make, both to ourselves or other people. A person with good self-respect is a person who makes good on their word – when they say they are going to be somewhere, they will be. If you are unable to commit to following through, then communicate that. If you are unsure and will know in a week whether you will be able to attend, then say that. Anything other than this might be you declining an invitation, but it is not you setting boundaries. Declining invitations is not an empowering decision if you had to lie in order to make that decision. Faking illness or making up imaginary plans is another way of avoiding communicating your needs and that is why it is important to be able to decline invites.

Saying yes to every invitation can often be a knee-jerk reaction. We check if we are free that night and if we are, we say yes. The step we are missing is actually asking ourselves if we want to attend. For me, I learnt this step when two of my parents' friends kept making condescending remarks about my job. My parents often visit them on our holidays together, and every time, there would be sarcastic comments questioning my competency, my success and whether it's a sustainable career path. For a few years I put up with it, but learning about boundaries meant I realized that just because I was on holiday with my family and my family wanted to see those friends, didn't mean I had to go with them. I told my parents that I didn't like being around these two friends and the reason why, and they understood. So on the evenings they would go out to see them, I would enjoy staying in the hotel room alone.

An important part of this was also realizing which element of this was within my control. It is not fair or right to control who my parents are friends with, and if they don't have an issue with their comments, then of course they feel no need to set a boundary around it. Their boundaries are allowed to be different to mine. However, comments about my job do cross my boundaries and I think it's vital to protect your energy. There were moments when my parents didn't understand why their friends' comments affected me so much or why I would choose to stay home instead of joining them, but it's not necessary for them to understand my boundaries as long as they respect them, and they do.

The beautiful side effect of only turning up when you want to is that people no longer take your presence for granted. On the nights when I would join my family, my dad started thanking me for joining them and it felt really good to be appreciated, as opposed to being expected to attend. It also means when you do turn up, it is a compliment to the host, as they know you are not attending out of obligation, but because you actually want to be in their company.

When I first started saying no to the invites, I started worrying that I was missing out. This is often labelled as FOMO ("fear of missing out"). You can't feel an emotion without a thought preceding it, and the thoughts I would have before I would feel FOMO were always the same two thoughts. The first thought would be that their evening was better than mine was. The cure to this is to remind yourself why you chose an evening in and the reasons you declined the event. Remind yourself that every time you say no to an event, you are actually saying yes to something else, and you can't enjoy the yes if you are focusing on the no. When you are mulling over whether you made the better choice out of two options, you ignore all the reasons you made the decision to begin with. Comparing the night you could have had to the night you did have just means you ignore the positives of the situation you chose. If you spend the night asking if you are missing out, you then miss out on what's actually going on right in front of you. The funny thing is that often, my friends would call the next day to say I didn't miss much. That led to the understanding that this comparison was simply an illusion. I can't physically be in two places at once, so there is no way to know whether I would actually have enjoyed that party. I declined it for a reason, whether that's because of the party itself or my need for alone time, and that reason was important when I made that decision.

The regret of making that decision is created out of making that party seem better than it probably was. Instead, start seeing alone time as a valid and equally important use of your time as being sociable.

The other thought that would lead to the FOMO feeling stemmed from the dread that all my friends were having fun without me, and more so, the completely irrational fear that if they had fun without me, they might realize that parties are better without me present, and stop inviting me altogether. All of this stemmed from being insecure in my relationships. As soon as I found friendships where I was constantly shown how much I was loved and appreciated, this thought disappeared. Finding people who love you, treat you well and respect your boundaries builds a stronger foundation for friendships and as a result, you stop seeing friendships as competitions. A friend enjoying time with other people is not a threat to your own relationship. The length of time spent together or the number of parties attended become irrelevant, and instead your focus switches to feeling connected when you do actually get to spend time together.

The flip side of this feeling that I often hear from clients is, "But she needs me there!" or "He is going to hate me if I don't show up." These thoughts are again based on assumptions and not reality. I was reminded of this when I said this exact sentence to my life coach, Michelle. My housemate wanted to throw a party at our place and every time we had thrown a party, we had both done it together. But on this occasion, the time of year she wanted to throw the party was when I was swamped with work and didn't have the energy to want to be at the party. So when Michelle suggested that my housemate go ahead with the party but I simply not attend, I retorted, "But she's never done it alone." Michelle flipped this mentality quickly by telling me that it was quite arrogant of me to assume the party would be no fun without me and that my housemate couldn't survive without my presence. Sometimes humans are a little guilty of thinking the whole world revolves around us and we place too much importance on other people's need for our attendance – this reminder made me fact-check this thought.

As long as you've addressed the hidden fears behind declining invitations, the only task left is to actually decline. In most cases when you decline an event, you don't need to give a reason. Sometimes, the person may respond asking for a reason and then you can decide if that's information they are entitled to, but from the outset we need to remove that idea that it is rude to decline unless you provide a reason. We need to eradicate the idea that being busy means another engagement. You could be busy that evening because you want to spend time alone. The problem with deciding your availability based on whether you have a space in your diary is that you are not actually choosing how to spend your time. You are allowing other people and your diary to dictate your schedule.

We live in a society that makes us believe our schedules should always be full and that an hour spent on the sofa alone watching TV is a waste of time. It tells us that a spare hour should be used productively, and that productive activities and commitments to others are more important than time alone. This is because society has glorified being busy. Our productivity is connected so heavily to our worth that when we slow down for a moment, not only do we have to process the feelings we are neglecting, but our self-esteem wanes without the constant busyness of our lives. Prioritizing alone time is an essential building block of loving yourself, because people who love themselves enjoy spending time with themselves. Treating the time with yourself with equal importance as your commitment to others is part of self-care. When you love yourself, you gain real ownership of your time and energy.

As much as we must learn how to decline invitations, we should also comprehend that not everyone *deserves* an invitation. We see this arise when people are trying to decide who is invited to their wedding, with family members interjecting that they *must* invite this person or that person. I found myself in a similar situation at my twenty-first birthday party. In my friendship group, twenty-first birthdays were a big deal. Everyone had decided to throw huge parties, the majority of which were black tie and elaborate affairs. My birthday fell in August, right after we had all graduated. In university, I had a huge friendship group of around 25 people, but by the end of third year, and definitely after graduation, there was no denying this friendship group was not one happy family but instead a bunch of fragments. For everyone else's twenty-first, they had invited the whole group indiscriminately but I couldn't bring myself to do that. I couldn't understand why I should invite someone who I haven't spoken to in the last year, much less someone who has actually been rude to me in the past, so I didn't. I invited who I wanted to and that was it. My friendship group had their reactions: some thought it was mean, some thought it caused unnecessary drama and others thought it was just awkward. But when I looked around the room on the day, it felt great to know every single person was in the room because I wanted them to be (and they wanted to be). Without the people who I didn't want in the room, all the competitiveness and cliquey dynamics were removed. It was worth making a few difficult decisions and having a few awkward conversations to have a day I could enjoy.

I want to challenge the idea that you should invite people that you don't want simply to be "polite" or to abide by old-fashioned etiquette. Is it really more polite to be invited but not wanted? We can get wrapped in "etiquette" for years. We've heard so many weird variations of "rules of politeness", but none are very logical. One of the rules I hear the most is that if they invite you, you must invite them – but you had no choice in whether they invited you and if they didn't want to invite you, they shouldn't have. The rule of always inviting family is also trotted out, but as the saying goes "You don't get to choose your family." However, you do get to choose who attends your events, and a family member who doesn't make an effort doesn't get a ticket into your life simply because you share blood. Another common rule I hear is around gifts – if they buy you an engagement present, for example, they earn an invite to a wedding. Gifts aren't meant to be in exchange for anything. A gift by definition is something given willingly without payment, so if a gift is given in the hopes of an invite, that's not a gift. Write them a thank-you card and move on.

Ignoring all the rules of etiquette and politeness will seem strange to some, and some might even call it selfish, so be prepared for people to have their reactions. But also be prepared to start enjoying your events so much more knowing that everyone in the room is someone you want to be there.

Take Action: Now that you prioritize yourself, I want you to start scheduling in your needs as if they are meetings with yourself. Like going to the gym? Put it into your diary as if it's evening plans with someone else. Been wanting to catch up on the latest episode of your favourite TV show? Put it into your calendar for an evening this week. If you've blocked the time out and someone suggests that night, it automatically becomes easier to say, "No, I'm busy, can we do the next night?" One of my friends, Jenny, likes to say, "Act like a VIP, get treated like a VIP." I say, "Treat yourself like a VIP and you'll become one."

Block, Mute, Delete: Determining Access

In society, we praise the length of friendships and admire those who are married for 50 years without stopping to question the quality of those relationships. We praise forgiveness to such a high extent that we are often left with relationships that have so much underlying resentment that bitching about your friends is normalized. When you learn healthy boundaries, this kind of normalized gossiping starts to feel toxic. Sigmund Freud is often quoted as having said, "Before you diagnose yourself with depression or low self-esteem, first make sure you are not surrounded by idiots." When you improve the quality of people in your life, your life will improve. In order to improve the quality of people in your life, you need to improve your quality of communication. Boundaries mean you grow in self-esteem and respect for yourself and talking behind people's backs no longer feels authentic. Learning how to communicate means you now have the skills to convey your discontent to someone's face – you go directly to the individual you have an issue with. When you see others are not doing the same, life can seem a little jarring.

The people in your life knew a different version of you, and not everyone adjusts well to the new version. In fact, a lot of people will prefer the old you and will try their hardest to drag you back there, so a compulsory part of incorporating boundaries into your life is determining who gets access to you. Since I've introduced boundaries into my life, I have become even more selective about who has access to me. You do not have to be at everyone else's disposal. One of the best ways to protect your energy and heart is to only give them to people who have earned them and have shown they can be trusted to be respectful of your space. The more self-development work you do, the more you might find that you are less accessible to other people.

I am a firm believer in the saying, "You are the five people you spend the most time with." It is inevitable that how someone speaks, how they act and how they treat you will have an effect on you, both consciously and unconsciously, and sometimes this personal growth results in you being misaligned in your friendship groups. There was a year in my life when I was learning boundaries that I now refer to as the "mass exodus" because so many people left my life that year. Have you ever had a friend who was constantly a mess? Their life always had drama and as soon as one thing got sorted, something else would fall apart. I was that friend, the friend that makes you feel better about your own life – until I started sorting my own life out. I finally faced all the medical trauma I'd been through, went to therapy, stopped dating men that were bad for me and actually found a career I was passionate about. In two short years, I turned my life around, and as a result all my friendship dynamics shifted. It's hard to change a friendship dynamic when so much of it was based on fixing a person who no longer needed fixing. I was surrounded by people with a saviour complex whose self-esteem depended on me being broken and who unconsciously liked the fact that I had no boundaries. They were so used to me making them my highest priority that when I started saying no, standing up for myself and not allowing them to take advantage of my time and energy, our relationships started to fragment. My taste in people changed. I outgrew the box they put me in.

There are two ways to change the amount of access a person has to you. You can either cut them out entirely or you can distance. The first people I did this with were my exes, and guys who would disappear and reappear at their convenience. This was them deciding access and determining that my company was only wanted when they were bored or horny, so I unfollowed all of them, deleted all their numbers and our messages. We are all guilty of rereading old messages, but that keeps you trapped in the old version of yourself and leaves no room for new people to enter your life. Once a romantic relationship ends or they ghost, they no longer get access to me. If you want to end things, you communicate it and if you are unable to do that, you do not get to return to my life.

This is a rule I keep to this day, and it was tested when a guy from my past reappeared on a dating app, asking me how I was. Looking at his message, it occurred to me that as much as I used to get annoyed at their entitlement for re-entering my life when they pleased, I needed to take accountability for the fact that I was letting them enter. While I don't believe in ghosting, I do believe in not accepting the initial message. So I hit decline, and it felt like me actively denying access to him, like a bouncer on the door of a club saying, "Oi, you can't come in." In a conversation, one person starts it, and the other person has to accept; a reply is an acknowledgement to agree to enter into that conversation. That's why in texting or any online communication, if my number is being used inappropriately because they have got it through a third party or you send a message because you have my number from our past, I am not obligated to reply. Ghosting is different because it happens mid-conversation or mid-relationship and it is a purposeful avoidance that occurs out of fear of having a difficult conversation. There is a difference between declining access from the outset and removing access without communicating that to the other party.

The next thing I did after deleting numbers and old messages was determining who had access to my information online. My online presence had been growing over the last few years and that meant anytime I went to a party with school friends and uni friends, I would get snarky comments asking if I had bought my followers, which I felt undermined the dream job I was creating. What I realized is the only reason these people knew so much information about my life was because of my Facebook. I had Facebook friends who I hadn't spoken to in years and who didn't even have my phone number yet could find out way more detail about me from my profile than any phone number would provide. While I couldn't make my Instagram account private because it was now part of my job, there was something

I could do to limit access to me on my private accounts. I created a new rule: anyone who I wouldn't want to have my phone number was not allowed on my private Instagram or Facebook page. The hardest part of this was when I decided to initiate this rule on my business Instagram account. I followed a number of people in the industry out of politeness and simply because we were in the same community. I would see them occasionally at events, but after a few years, I hated my own newsfeed as it was cluttered with content I didn't like, so I extended this rule to my work account.

When I did this, an unexpected side effect was the number of people noticing. Since I had already done this on my private accounts and hadn't received any messages, I assumed it was something people didn't notice, but I guess there is a difference when you are an influencer and the number of people who follow you affects your job. It puzzled me though because I received these messages within a few hours of unfollowing and shortly found out it was due to an app. Why anyone would have an app on their phone to track a figure that can only upset them baffles me, but regardless, it gave me the opportunity to have more difficult conversations to navigate.

When given this opportunity, a number of people make up white lies, or worse, they claim it was a mistake and begrudgingly hit follow to avoid the hard conversations but again, this is not living life with integrity or according to your needs. Instead, I explained to each person what they wanted to know and answered their questions about whether I was angry with them or whether something had happened. It hadn't, I had simply changed what kind of content I wanted to be seeing and wished them well. When it was the case, I reassured them that our relationship was still the same, but online, I was building different boundaries. Throughout this process, one person sticks out the most as having the most difficulty understanding how I could still think fondly of them but not want to see their content.

I knew she had been worrying about it through a friend but because I don't like having conversations via a third party, I told the person who told me that if she had an issue to bring it up with me directly. I didn't hear anything more for a few months until we both found ourselves at the same event. I thought the conversation may come up, but it didn't; we had a lovely time together and the next morning I received a message that read, "I have something to tell you, don't be anxious, I did a silly human thing." Boundaries are so uncomfortable for a lot of people, mainly because they are not used to it, and even in this message, I could tell it took a lot of vulnerability for her to reach out. Whenever you communicate boundaries, do so with as much compassion as possible.

Her text continued:

> "So I saw you unfollowed me and I took it personally and when I was drunk, I unfollowed you but I didn't mean it and I didn't want to refollow you and for you to see it and think 'Wow, petty,' so I'm going to follow you again, OK? I'm sorry, it's so stupid because I'm a grown-up and obviously you have a super good reason for doing it, which you really don't have to tell me at all, but saying this made me feel like I just exhaled."

I hold a lot of respect for anyone who has the courage to start a hard conversation, especially when it is clear this is not their norm. I wanted to make sure my reply demonstrated that respect, gave her enough explanation to give her closure and also reassured her worries about our relationship, so I replied with the following:

"I am so glad you feel so much better and thank you for sharing how you feel with me! It wasn't personal, I unfollowed 600 people. I unfollowed nearly everyone who posts about body positivity and fashion because a large part of my job is already so focused on bodies, that I didn't want it in my newsfeed as well. Ultimately, I haven't been insecure about my body in five years and so that content doesn't help me anymore. I found reading about other people's bodies just emphasizes the idea that we are just our bodies and I believe we are more than that. Your content is wonderful and will help so many people who are in the early stages, and I needed accounts like yours in the beginning of my journey, too, so keep doing what you are doing! I only want you to follow me if you actually like my content. If the only reason you are following me is because I followed you, then that's not a reason to follow someone. You can text me anytime and I still love you. I am concerned that you have been worrying about this for so long. Next time, I would love it if you could just ask me. I will always be honest, and that way you don't have to sit in that shit feeling."

A lot of people will think having to go through these difficult conversations is not worth the hassle. For you, that very
well might be the case, especially if following people that
make you unhappy doesn't disrupt your day, but for me it
was more on principle. Why was I letting people whom I
had only met a handful of times decide what was on my
newsfeed? If I was honest with myself, the only reason I
worried about unfollowing was because I worried about
what people thought. I also considered how it would affect
my work opportunities to not be following people in my
community, but fact-checking these thoughts also meant
realizing none of these people had actually ever supported
me in my career. These were just connections that they used
whenever they needed something from me. They were one-
way relationships, and even if they were only work acquaintances, it didn't align with the new life I was building.

Similar changes also started happening in my real life
with old friends. In our society, we keep relationships in
our life as a default. Society doesn't teach us that we are
allowed to re-evaluate our relationships over time to see
if they are healthy for both parties. Ask yourself how that
person makes you feel. It is easy to focus on the small
moments where they were loving and supportive, but try
to contextualize this within the lifespan of your entire relationship. Look at your dynamic as a whole to see how they
make you feel the majority of the time. When you are truly
choosing a friendship, be aware that both distancing and
cutting people out are options. Don't keep a relationship

simply because it is old. A good friend is better than an old friend.

The question you need to ask yourself is if the good outweighs the bad. Of course, friendships and relationships go in phases where they need your support more than you need theirs, but overall, it should come out equal. People in your life should never make you feel bad on purpose and if they do that unintentionally, you should be able to voice your concern and resolve it. If they are unable to do that, this is when I would begin to question whether they deserve a place in my life.

The decision between whether to cut someone out completely or to distance comes down to whether the dynamic has become a toxic one or whether you are in different phases of your life. I want to emphasize that distancing is not the consolation prize you settle for when you are too scared to cut someone out. If you would describe a relationship as toxic, then the person needs to be cut out. If the dynamic is simply unhealthy, then just take some space. The health of a relationship can fluctuate, but a toxic dynamic is due to ingrained patterns that will only change when they want to change – not when you want them to.

Distancing

When it comes to distancing, this often happens organically in friendships. This could be due to loss of common interests or simply the fact that there is a change in life that makes it less convenient to meet up and see each other. If the friendship matters enough, you will make that additional effort, but without the close physical proximity, you come to see that not everyone is worth that effort. This is a normal part of life. There is also intentional distancing.

When I first moved to London, I found myself in a friendship group I didn't choose to be in. I was good friends with three of the group, but the other two were complete strangers to me. I was so used to hanging out with the three as a foursome and this new dynamic was an adjustment that left me always feeling like the odd one out. Everyone in the group was in long-term relationships, and I found myself feeling bad about being single every time I was around them. On the whole, I was happy being single, but within this group, there was a "poor Michelle" dynamic that I believe made them feel superior to me. Alongside this, my social media profile was growing, and every dinner seemed to involve a passive-aggressive joke about me and my followers. I knew I wanted out of this friendship group, but I still wanted to stay friends with the three I had chosen as friends, so I distanced myself. I declined all group invitations and for a few months, I didn't see any of them. Eventually, with two of them, I eased back into monthly dinners one on one and that suited me so much more.

Outside of the group dynamic, there was no competition and I felt more connected having individual dinners anyway. The third friend was actually the one I was closest to, but we never found our way back to seeing each other alone. We had been best friends in university and even went travelling to Japan for a month, just the two of us. But for a year or two after that distancing, we would only see each other at parties – until one party last year when we found ourselves on a sofa together catching up properly. The next morning, I woke up feeling great about our catch-up but also having a seed of doubt in my mind that it could have just been because we were drunk. A few days later, I still felt the same, so I sent her a simple text saying:

> "Was lovely seeing you on Saturday. Let's have dinner soon!"

She responded:

> "Babes, you too! Have thought about you lots since. Absolutely!"

In the space of a few months, we were back to seeing each other. We have spoken about it since, and we both said it was nice how we were able to take space from one another in an undramatic way and when we were ready, we just picked up where we left off. The love was never lost between the two of us. We just were in different places in our life. Distancing allows for this and I am convinced that if I hadn't taken the space when I needed it, passive aggression and snarky side comments would have done damage that would have meant there would have been no relationship to return to. It made me realize that distancing was not only the healthiest option but the more loving, kind and compassionate option.

In other situations, distancing is done with a conversation. One situation in my own life where this happened was with a friend who I found myself constantly bickering with. It would always be silly and pedantic things. We were best friends, seeing each other multiple times a week, and it got to a point where I started questioning whether we were actually bickering because we were seeing each other too much. We had the familiarity of sisters – and squabbled like sisters, too. The breaking point was when we were in a group of our friends and they got sick of us picking on each other. Once we left the group, another friend suggested that we just need a little space, so I spoke to her about it. We both agreed to cut down our contact, and that it would do our relationship good. It lasted for a few months, but as soon as we started seeing each other more, we started arguing again, so we tried a new rule. I realized that every time we bickered, it would always start with a text message, so our new rule was that we would stop texting and only call each other. It makes me laugh that people think boundaries are about ruining a relationship because in so many ways, it is actually the opposite – you are trying your best to fix a relationship. Again, this lasted a few months and it worked until one day, we had to text and fell right back into our old pattern. I couldn't keep arguing. I said I wanted to take a proper pause from our relationship and not talk to each other for a few months. My friend refused; she said if we stop being friends, then that's it, forever. It was her right to set her own boundary, and that left me with a decision to make. She wanted to keep trying to fix it and I didn't. I wanted us to be friends in the future and she didn't. I told her that I loved her and that I always would, but I couldn't keep arguing the way we were, and that if we were both honest, it was unhealthy for the both of us. Unfortunately, distancing sometimes leads to someone being cut out completely and as much as I didn't want it to be forever, that was her decision to make and I have to respect that.

This year, I had a similar situation occur though where distancing was simply distancing. One of my best friends and I had a bad fight. We had never argued before and she was actually the friend who I used to say was the best example of boundaries. The stress of coronavirus had changed our dynamic and the increased levels of stress had changed our communication. We were both known for our honesty but over the course of a few months in lockdown, on both sides, we failed to wrap our honesty in compassion and would both often deliver our honesty in an unnecessarily blunt way. This communication issue reached boiling point the first time we were able to see each other after lockdown. The fight was short, sudden and ended with one of us crying, one of us raising our voice and a slammed door. The next day, she texted wanting to resolve it but also asked that if I was still emotional, to not reply because she was too vulnerable to hear it so I sent the following reply:

"Thank you for the voicenote. I'm still angry. I want to resolve this but I am submitting my book today so I'm focusing on that. I'm going to take the weekend but will get back to you on Monday. Good luck with your packing and have a safe flight xx"

On Monday, I stuck to my promise of getting back to her. I knew I was still angry, I knew that what she had done was not intentional but my trust was still broken and I needed time to heal so I asked for that.

"I'm going to be honest in saying I'm still angry but I promised a reply today so I wanted to get back to you. My trust is very broken and I don't know where we go from here. I love you and I want to mend this but I think we both need space from this relationship. Could we check in with each other next month? Xx"

We had a brief conversation to provide us both with a little understanding and then she agreed and sent the following:

"I'm glad we had this conversation. It brought me some clarity. Now let's take some time to heal/process and also think about how we can prevent this happening again in the future. I love you lots, hope you enjoy your birthday and I will talk to you next month xx"

We took the space. We healed and time apart was exactly what we needed. The following month, we texted each other to arrange to meet up and whilst we both acknowledged it would take time to fully build trust with each other again, a few months on, we are now stronger than we were before. When you start intentionally distancing, there is no way to know how it will end but what I believe is that the right relationships end up getting stronger and the relationships that weren't meant to be, leave your life.

Cutting people out

When it comes to cutting people out, it is usually because I have tried to work on the relationship multiple times, both communicating my issues and giving them the chance to change their behaviour. If this is not done, cutting people out becomes my reinforcement of my boundaries. This is never out of blame, but more so an understanding that we both can't provide each other with what we need. In rare instances, cutting people out has happened over one disagreement where such hurtful words were said that the trust and respect was broken. If you do decide to cut someone out, this should always be communicated. If you've ever had respect for them, then end the friendship with respect as well. Having higher standards for the people in your life also means you need to start behaving at a higher standard. Ghosting isn't a behaviour that warrants my respect or one that I would feel proud of myself for. When someone doesn't have the decency to end a relationship, I believe they never had any respect for me. Even if you no longer care about the other person anymore, it's cruel, unkind and shows no consideration for the mutual memories that you share.

One memory where I cut someone out over a singular incident was in the middle of a birthday party where weight loss was being discussed. I was trying to explain my point of view that health is not an appearance and that a lot of medicines and illnesses lead to weight gain, so you should not judge someone's body. The conversation escalated quickly from a hypothetical conversation about a news article to a real conversation about my own weight and health. I excused myself from the table because, as I advise my clients, you do not need to stay in the room for body-shaming conversations. I was so upset that my friend had decided to body shame me publicly in a conversation with strangers

I didn't know, that I decided to go home. I told the host I was leaving, didn't tell her the reasoning as I didn't want to involve her on her birthday and hoped that tomorrow, when my friend had sobered up, it would resolve itself. On the way out, she stopped me and told me to "Stop being so sensitive" about my weight and that it was "time to wake up". I ignored the comment, gave her the benefit of the doubt and hoped it was just the alcohol. The next morning, I woke up to a voicemail that not only continued the same conversation from the night before but also used all the vulnerable information I had told her in our friendship to undermine both my career and my romantic relationship. This friend was about 30 years older than me, and we had quite a mother-daughter dynamic where I would often seek comfort or advice when I was confused about a situation, and she had used all that information in an emotionally abusive way.

The strange thing was that we had been friends for over five years, and I was the same weight I was when we met. Nothing about my body had changed, but something about her own body image clearly had. Wondering whether she held these thoughts the entire length of our friendship is a thought that I couldn't get out of my head. That, combined with the voicemail, meant the trust had been broken in a way it could never be mended. I also didn't want to mend it. I sent her a text to communicate the end of our friendship and we haven't spoken since. In hindsight, there were probably warning signs that she secretly held these thoughts about my body, one of them being that every time we saw each other she would compliment me by saying that I had lost weight, even though I never had but I didn't know enough about boundaries then to be conscious enough to notice red flags.

Ending friendships is always sad. Especially when it ends in a way that you never could have foreseen. An essential part of this process is allowing yourself that sadness and the grief. "Grief" is a word that is often only used in the context of death, but it is an emotion humans can have around any loss. It can surface not only when you end a friendship, but also when you lose the person they used to be. You are allowed to miss them. That is not proof that they deserve to be back in your life, it is simply proof that you loved them at one time and you miss the person they used to be. You may also miss how they used to make you feel and your memories together. Allow yourself to heal, grieve the loss and process the sadness while also recognizing that you have made the healthiest decision. As long as you have not cut someone out in anger or haste, your decision would have been carefully deliberated, so do not use their absence as a way to romanticize what the relationship used to be.

Letting old friends back in your life

Every time I talk about cutting people out, I am asked if I have ever let someone back into my life. I'm not a fan of revolving doors. When I shut a door on a relationship, that door remains closed. I believe there is a reason why it ended, and because I terminated the relationship properly with good boundaries and a calm approach, I have never had regrets. In all the relationships I have ended, I have only brought one person back into my life, and the main reason for that is because we didn't end it properly. This was long before I knew about boundaries and before I had even graduated university. It was actually done in the exact opposite way I teach people to do it now – it ended in a screaming match between me and my other three housemates, all throwing insults at each other. That fight was full of regrettable moments for me, not only in how it was handled but also some of the things I said. The evening that it happened, I actually remember promising myself that I would never speak to another person like that again. Seven years later, I have stuck to that promise and never raised my voice at a friend since. As I said above, things go wrong, and sometimes you have to learn a lesson the hard way. That was the first and last time I have yelled at a friend.

Despite the fact the fight was between all four of us living together, there was only one friendship that I often thought about. But it would take two years for us to find ourselves in the same room, or actually, in the same queue for a club. We had both been invited to a birthday party and I found myself standing next to her waiting to get in. She said hi, I said hi back and we left it at that but the moment I saw her, all I could think about was how much I missed her. So with a little alcohol in me, I walked straight up to her and said just that: "I miss you." She hugged me and told me she missed me too and asked if we could go have a chat. We ended up finding a private room in the back of the club and talked through every single thing that happened in that argument two years before.

We both had a lot to get off our chest and the two years that had passed had certainly helped us both to think more clearly about the situation. She acknowledged that she had been really stressed in the lead-up to exams and that led to her acting out of character, and I acknowledged my part in it. Namely, that I had been diagnosed with PTSD a few months before and hadn't been coping well with it. We both spoke about how the dynamic of that flat was incredibly toxic and how it impacted our friendship, and that when things in the flat changed and the dynamic became all three of them against me, I felt attacked. We hashed out every element of that fight and we both apologized for our parts in it, only to surface three hours later to discover we were the only people in the club and everyone else had left ages ago.

We have spoken about this conversation since and we both think we wouldn't have had the friendship we have today without resolving all those issues. We were both hurt by the words that were said in the argument with our flatmates, and in order to truly put it behind us, we needed to go through that situation with a fine-tooth comb. It's funny how you remember every word that was said, even two years later, when hurtful words came out of the mouth of someone who you loved. There is no way we could have pretended that fight never happened. At the same time and in many ways, we built a new friendship rather than trying to fix the old one. We gave each other the permission to be new people and acknowledged that we didn't really know each other anymore. We started our friendship from scratch and we built it back up gradually, slowly earning each other's trust until now, five years later, we are as close as we were back then. We are now at the point where I would call her one of my best friends. But this did not happen overnight and it would not have been healthy or safe to jump back to where we left off. Healing the friendship did not mean automatic re-entry to every part of my life. It was careful and conscious baby steps so that the trust could grow slowly.

Another element that was important was the amount of time that had passed. Since we had been friends in university, we had both graduated, moved to different parts of the country, had partners and gone through the really transformative experience of leaving education and going into the "real world" of work. We had both changed and become different people. A lot of the time when friendships end, one party wants the other to change when the other party isn't ready. We both went our separate ways, did our personal growth work and then came together.

While this was clearly the journey we were both meant to go on, it's important to recognize that this situation could have been avoided. Before that "breaking point" fight, there were many missed opportunities to set boundaries. What happened here might have been cutting someone out, but it wasn't setting boundaries. It was a lack of boundaries that led to an eruption of emotion. It is only when you cut someone out from a place of negative emotions that you will grow to regret it. I truly believe that if you cut someone out properly (and not the way I did to this friend), there is rarely a reason you want them back in your life. I hope that with the tools provided in this book and the examples of how not to do it, you can learn from my mistakes just as I have.

But they are a good person

Whenever I talk about access, cutting people out and distancing, the most common response I get is, "What do I do if the person is a good person?" People will send me paragraphs about how kind and well-meaning the other party is and that's great, but that is not a reason to keep someone in your life. You don't build a fence between you and your neighbour because you hate your neighbour, you do it because you need your own space. In fact, it has little to do with your neighbour at all – and boundaries work in the same way. Cutting people out is about me, not them. It's about what I want, not about what they lack. In society, when relationships end, romantic or platonic, we have a tendency to demonize the other party in order to heal, but it doesn't need to be that extreme. They don't need to have bitched about me or screwed me over in some dramatic way in order for the relationship to not be healthy anymore. The people I set boundaries with are not evil and the people I cut out are not always toxic. In fact, a lot of people I have cut out, I still love. I still care about them and wish them well and will ask about them if they come up in conversation, but it doesn't mean I want them in my life. Someone doesn't have to be a bad person in order for them to be bad for you.

But what if they are in a bad place?

I often get asked whether you should be more forgiving if someone is in a bad place. As in the example above, I was in a bad place when that argument happened and while that was the only relationship that ended as a result of my PTSD, it was not the only relationship that was affected by it. When I was struggling with it, I said a lot of hurtful words, and sometimes the damage you do is irreparable. You can apologize, but you are not owed forgiveness. That is a huge part of accountability. I personally do not believe mental illness is an excuse to be an arsehole to anyone. Being in a bad place may be the reason, but it should never be used as an excuse or to avoid accountability with an apology. We hurt people we love all the time, and sometimes those words have permanent consequences. We have to live with those consequences, even if that means someone else not wanting you in their life anymore, because part of having good boundaries is respecting their decision. In situations where the other party is the one in the bad place, I would look at their ability to take responsibility and whether they are changing their behaviour or repeatedly using their mental health difficulties to not respect your wishes. This is a decision only you can make and each context will be different, but in my life, it often comes down to how I am being treated and not allowing people to treat me a certain way, regardless of the reason.

The loneliness that follows

When you cut out a lot of people, it is normal to feel loneliness. Some of that will be grief that is surfacing around your losses. There will also be moments where you will miss them, and some of that will be your discomfort at being alone. Loneliness is a key part you have to sit through and process. If you avoid it, loneliness becomes a reason to avoid removing other toxic dynamics in your life. The thinking is that you don't want to feel more lonely, so you don't remove the people you should from your life, but this is not the solution. In fact, the times when I have felt loneliness aren't when I have been alone but actually when I am in a room full of people who don't understand me. Being alone and being lonely are two distinct things. While you might think that keeping those toxic dynamics around will help avoid loneliness, what you are actually avoiding is being by yourself.

Learning how to be alone is a necessary life skill. It was only in this space created by cutting people out that I realized the reason I hated being alone so much is because I didn't like myself. The only way you truly love yourself is if you know yourself, and the only way you can get to know yourself is spending time with yourself. People who love themselves enjoy their own company, and all this empty space in my life gave me the opportunity to learn how to do this. Initially, it had to be quite intentional: I would create little dates for myself or spend an afternoon doing an activity alone that I would normally do with a friend. I would have to force myself to carve out time in my diary for me time. It was very conscious, and I put in the extra effort that I would if I was doing it with a friend.

For example, if I was watching TV alone, it would usually be on my computer propped on my lap, but if a friend was coming over for a movie, I would get some fun snacks and make the effort to plug my laptop into the TV, so I started doing that even when I was alone. It might seem small and insignificant, but it teaches you that you are just as worthy of the effort made for friends. Over time, creating that space in your life – and in the meantime, working on enjoying your own company – means you leave space for new people to enter your life. You will find new people, I promise. And when you do, you'll be shocked when you find yourself choosing a night in alone, when you once would have dreaded the thought.

Take Action: When you cut someone out of your life, it can be painful. In my grieving process, I always find writing a few lists helps to make sure it doesn't happen again. Try making lists yourself using the following headings to work through the process of cutting someone out:

1) Red flags that I missed
2) The changes in the relationship that I did not notice
3) What I wish I could have done differently
4) What I have learnt from the relationship
5) Lessons I will take into my other relationships

All of these lists should be used to help you understand the relationship and to be able to grow from this situation. It allows you to take the lessons you need, and if you are able to learn from it, that helps the healing process. What these lists shouldn't be used for is blame and regret. Your relationship served a purpose at the time and just because it no longer exists doesn't mean it was a waste of time. It is possible to end a relationship and also acknowledge that that person once was a good family member, friend or partner to you. Spending your time wishing you had learnt those lessons before you did is pointless. You couldn't have known what you didn't know then. These lists are there to help ensure it won't happen again, not only because you will have a list of warning signs and red flags when meeting new people, but also you will be able to notice changes in your current relationships that you might have been ignoring in the past. An essential part of building up your voice and your self-esteem is ensuring you are kind to yourself throughout this.

I Don't Want to Talk About it: Limiting Information

I learned the importance of limiting information via the internet. Having a public following has meant that a comment I receive a lot is "I know so much about you". In reality, you know only what I allow you to know. My following started six years ago when I went viral for a campaign I created called Scarred Not Scared, which discusses body image around surgery scars. I didn't expect for it to get much attention, let alone to go viral and my bikini picture to be in the news, plastered across magazines and newspapers, but the aspect I definitely didn't foresee was that I would be asked endlessly why my surgery scars exist. Those scars were created out of my most traumatic memories and having to reel off that I had undergone 15 surgeries, a brain tumour, a punctured intestine, an obstructed bowel, a cyst in my brain and a condition called hydrocephalus in every interview for the last five years started to wear on me. My career as an influencer essentially started with me sharing my trauma, and learning how to boundary that was definitely a trial by fire. My medical record becoming public knowledge meant that people felt entitled to dig into other parts of my life and as a result, I realized I needed to protect myself more. Boundaries created that protection that I needed.

Just because someone asks for information doesn't mean I have to provide it. More than that, just because I have previously provided that information doesn't mean that I have to repeat it or have the same conversation over and over again. My trauma is mine, which means I get to choose if, when and how much of it I want to share. I am also entitled to changing my mind and changing my boundaries as I evolve. I can make once-public information private again or probably more practically, I can navigate these conversations by directing them to the place where I have already discussed this in depth: my first book. I started using one sentence more than ever – "I don't want to talk about that" – and whenever I was asked for further details about my medical trauma, I would simply respond, "All the information you are looking for is in my first book."

When we lack confidence, we let others lead the conversation. But conversations are a two-way process, and if one person does not want to be a part of the conversation, they are entitled to not only say so, but step away from the conversation if the other party continues to force their agenda.

When working with clients with body-confidence issues, I strongly suggest they limit the number of diet conversations they are involved in. Diet culture has become part of our everyday language and when people are trying to grow their confidence in their appearance, it can be hard to build their self-esteem when so many of our daily conversations revolve around insulting ourselves and talking about weight loss. In these situations, I remind my clients that you do not have to participate in the conversation and that sitting there in silence is the best first step.

I used this in my own life with two of my friends and it is remarkable how noticeable it is. Both of these friends were much older than me and both had teenage kids. One day, one of them asked me for advice on her teenage daughter who had started hiding chocolate bars. I gave her my best body-confidence advice and then, out of curiosity, asked why she had asked me instead of our other friend, who actually has kids.

"Whenever we talk badly about our bodies, you never join in," she said.

"You noticed that?" I asked.

"Yes," she continued, "and even when we encourage you, you change the conversation."

We had all been friends for three years, and even though it had never been a conversation, it had been noticed.

When silence doesn't work, I suggest my clients say, "Can we change the conversation to something more interesting?" If they refuse to change the conversation, then I would be more concerned that your friend would like to talk about what they want to talk about, with no care about how that is affecting the company they are in. If you could have the conversation with someone else, why would you want to continue it when you are clearly affecting someone who is working on their personal development? As I mentioned previously, their response is most telling about the quality of the relationship.

In addition to silence or asking to change the conversation, you also have the option to leave the conversation. You do not need to stay in a conversation to be insulted. At first, this often seems like a daunting task. But you don't need to leave the conversation in a confrontational way, you can simply state that you are going to get a drink or go to the bathroom. As your confidence grows, you might find yourself setting a boundary by asking the other party to stop commenting on your body. Which tactic I use depends on the party involved, and how much energy I have. Sometimes I would rather just excuse myself and other times, especially when it is a repeat offender, I will set a firm boundary and state that if they continue to comment on my body, I will be walking away. Having set this boundary for over five years now, body-shaming comments that used to be a daily occurrence have now gone down to zero. I don't know whether it's because they get bored of me walking away mid-conversation or because they have lost hope of me ever changing, but the reason doesn't matter. What matters is that boundaries work.

Similarly, I have had to limit receiving information as well. A friend of mine was in a toxic relationship, and she agreed that he was toxic, but would often leave only to return to him shortly after. In the meantime, I would listen to her go through the whole breakup process again and again, reminding her that she'd said this before and asking what was different this time. She would continually say that this time was the end, but after a point, it felt like our conversations were reinforcing this pattern and I didn't want to be a part of it. In these conversations, every time I said anything, she would defend him. It started to feel to me like I was pushing her back into his arms, so after the third breakup, I told her I couldn't have this conversation again. We stayed friends, but they would continue to break up and make up for another year. In the meantime, she would not discuss it with me. If it came up accidentally, as it once did when I asked where she was and she was at his house, she would reply, "You don't want to know," and we would move on. In a situation like this, a lot of people would say that I should have tried to make or convince her to leave her relationship, but part of having healthy boundaries is respecting other people's decisions even if you would not make the same choice, and allowing others to make their own mistakes. It is an illusion to think that I could have done anything to make her leave that relationship before she was ready.

Who gets to know what?

One of the best ways to decide how much information a person is privy to is to look at your life and create levels of knowledge. I used to be the person who had 30 best friends, but keeping up that much contact is not realistic and sharing that extent of information with everyone is not safe. My levels are now 'best friends', 'good friends' and 'friends'. Best friends can become good friends and acquaintances can become friends. Having this criteria means that you can evaluate your friendships and not be stuck in the past of how close you used to be. A guy I once dated had different criteria for 'friends', 'mates' and 'acquaintances' but whatever label you use, it's the difference in closeness that matters.

When I bring up this idea of having levels of closeness, the main pushback I receive is that people feel dishonest by holding back information and in turn feel like they are holding back pieces of themselves. For those people, I say it is important to learn the difference between privacy and honesty. You are not being dishonest, you are choosing to keep some things private and that doesn't mean it has to be private indefinitely, but just for a certain period of time.

To use an example, my best friends and good friends knew I was writing a book about boundaries. When I got my first meeting with a publisher, I told my best friends. As soon as I got an offer but it wasn't signed, I told good friends. When it was all signed off, then I was ready to mention it to friends. With my best friends and good friends, I would start a conversation by saying, "I got an offer on my book!", whereas with a friend I would wait until we were having a conversation and they asked me what I was up to. It wasn't the fact that I thought my friends wouldn't be happy for me. I wouldn't be friends with someone who couldn't be happy for me, but when you share information, you open yourself up to external opinions. Sometimes I'm not ready to hear other people's thoughts about my decisions. I learnt this lesson with my first book. It took me four years to get published and especially towards the end of that road, there were friends who on the day I got 20 rejections, told me, "This is not the time to quit, this is the time to push harder." There were also friends that said, "Why don't you shelve it for a few years and come back to it later on?" It was not the fact that one was a good friend and one was a bad friend, but that one was a cautious person and the other was more stubborn in persisting in the face of failure. What I needed to remember was that neither had read the book, so their comments weren't a judgement of my work – one friend didn't want to see me quit and one didn't want to see me keep getting hurt. One opinion helped me and one opinion didn't, so when you boundary information, you also boundary opinions that can affect your own view.

If you confuse privacy with honesty, there will be a tendency to overshare. An overindulgence of information is often used to create a bond earlier than is safe, and is actually a protection mechanism to avoid the vulnerable stages of building a new relationship. We think that if we overshare personal information or pieces of our trauma, it will cement the relationship faster. The healthier approach is to share information in small ways, see if they can be trusted with that information and if so, then give more information. Using the example of my book deal above, I told someone my good news and the first question they asked was how much money I got for the deal. It felt awful. It felt like my accomplishment was meaningless unless it was proven financially. Because they were in the same industry as me, it made me think that what they were actually asking was how much they would be able to get for a book deal, rather than focusing on my accomplishment. This experience gave me vital information on whether I should share good news with them again. I would have much rather learned that lesson with something comparatively small rather than jumping into the emotional deep end and realizing that it was more shallow than I thought.

We often talk about the concept of an inner circle, but what I have found is that there are several levels of the inner circle, and each level comes with certain criteria. Everyone's criteria differs, but in my life, it revolves largely around the amount of time I spend with the person and the effort we go to see each other regularly. For me, a best friend is someone who I see once a week or once every two weeks. They stay over often and when they do, they sleep in my bed. I tell them everything and they are the first people I want to tell when I have good news. If I have an emergency, I can call them and rely on them to be there no matter what time of the day I call. In this category, you should have about a handful of people. Oftentimes, people get insecure around the fact that they can only name two or three. If you have two or three, that is enough. It is really hard to find this level of friendship and to maintain the closeness. Good friends are people I see once a month, they stay over occasionally but when they do, they sleep in the guest room. I will only tell them my happy news once it's confirmed, and if I am upset, I would be able to tell them that but I wouldn't call them in an emergency. In this group there should be around 10 people. In the category of "friends" are the people who I go for lunch with once every few months, they don't stay over unless there is a reason to. We go out on the town, I will invite them to events like a house party or even my work events, but we rarely go out for meals just the two of us. I will not make a particular effort to inform them of good news. If it comes up, I will mention it but I only tell them things that I would be happy with the whole world knowing. Acquaintances are the colleagues who I see at work events or the people I know online who I interact with every now and again.

Similarly, a best friend might know about every date I go on and will probably be the person who has my GPS location pin to check I am safe on a first date, whereas a good friend might only find out about the person I'm dating by the time of date two or three. You get to decide how many friends you have in each category and how you discuss your life with them. For me, my personal space and my apartment are really sacred, which is why I have differentiators for that, but if that doesn't matter to you, then that might not be one of yours. What matters is that there are delineations, but what those are between the subsections is your choice.

Take Action: Create your own inner-circle chart. Differentiate between various relationships and decide on the proximity you allow each person in your life. This might seem like a formulaic way of looking at your life, but it is useful to look at where people stand – whether your relationships are reciprocal, and who can be relied upon. It does not mean people stay in their category forever or that you have to physically move their name from one list to another every time a relationship progresses or changes, but it is a useful exercise to assess your life and an exercise you can return to if you start to question whether a relationship is becoming out of balance.

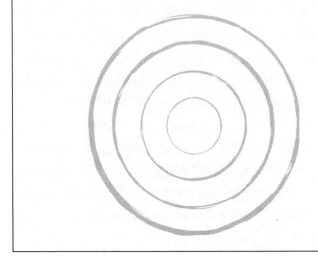

This is What I Need: The Flip Side of Boundaries

We have a weird concept in society that if someone knows you well enough, they should be able to anticipate your every need ("I shouldn't have to ask!"), and if they are unable to, then that demonstrates a lack of attention and care. This is inaccurate. As human beings, we assume the world thinks like we do. So if you are a particularly affectionate person who likes hugs when you are upset, you will try to comfort an upset loved one in a way that would comfort you. The thought "What would help me in this situation?" comes into your mind and you act in the same way. The problem with this is that all humans are different and while a hug might comfort you, your loved one might be sitting there wanting to talk about it.

When I was going through PTSD, I didn't want anyone to ask me about it. In fact, when I asked my parents if they could pay for my therapy, I said to them, "Something is wrong. I don't want to talk about it, but I need money to talk to someone else about it." That is how I work. That is what I need when my mental health is bad. In fact, I'm still like that to this day. I don't need to talk about it to anyone other than my life coach. The way my friends can help me is by talking to me about anything that doesn't involve my mental-health situation. For example, when I was in hospital, the thing that helped me most was when my friends would rant about their boy problems, as if they weren't Skyping me from a hospital bed halfway across the world.

So when my friend was going through her worst mental health struggle, what do you think I did? Bombard her with stories of my bad first dates and asked her about everything BUT her mental health. Months had passed and suddenly one day, in the middle of me chatting about some guy, she blurted out, "Are we just going to keep pretending that nothing has changed? Out of all my friends, I thought you would be most comfortable about talking about mental health and you've never even asked once!"

Whoa. I had got this so wrong. There were many assumptions that had taken place. I had assumed that she knew she could talk to me. Because she hadn't spoken to me about it, I had assumed she didn't want to. And meanwhile, she had assumed that I didn't want to talk about it because I was uncomfortable or I didn't care. A whole bunch of assumptions could have been avoided if I had said one simple sentence: "I'm here to talk. How can I help?"

Now, I always ask how I can help before jumping to conclusions and do my best to boundary my own opinion unless the person is specifically asking for it. I ask if they want me to listen, help them find a solution or provide advice. Some people just want to vent and some people want to actually know my opinion and clarifying this helps a lot. Also, since I am quite a blunt person, I tend to preface any honest advice with "Do you want me to be honest?" Most of the time, they say yes because when they come to me, they know what they are getting. But some of the time, I get a no, and when I do, I respect that. In a recent instance, a friend had gotten back with an ex. I asked her if she wanted me to be honest and she replied, "No, I want to enjoy this. I'll come back for honesty when this all ends badly." A sign of bad boundaries would have been pushing my own agenda of wanting to protect her from the pain of going through the breakup for the second time. Good boundaries mean understanding she is an adult who can make her own decisions. The fact that I believed it was the wrong decision doesn't make it so. Even if it was, people need to make their own mistakes. You can't force someone to learn a lesson they aren't ready to learn yet.

Asking for what you need seems basic, but the reason why most of us don't do it is because it requires vulnerability. Our rationale is that if we ask for what we need, and they don't give it to us, then it will be hurtful and that pain will be greater because we've just put our neck on the line to ask for something. In reality, our games – where we assume they should know what we need and then berate them for not being able to guess our needs – lead to more arguments and confusion. Someone can't know what they don't know. A classic example of this is the parent who unloads the dishwasher every day with building resentment until one day they snap and shout, "You are all so ungrateful! No one ever helps me unload the dishwasher!", and the family sit there confused because no one knew that they wanted help.

The way to avoid that resentment building up is to simply ask. I've seen this exact situation with adult housemates where they play games of waiting to see how long it takes

another housemate to realize the dishwasher needs empty-
ing, to use it as proof that they are the one that empties the
dishwasher more than the other. Wouldn't it be simpler to
just ask for what you need? But it's scary – and what if you
don't get what you need and they don't change their behaviour? Well, you've already skipped ahead a step and decided
how this conversation is going to end before you've already
had it. I know, because I've done it before.

I remember the vulnerability that was required when I
asked my housemate if we could spend more time together.
My housemate and I had lived together for seven years. I
was closer to her than my own sister, but in the last two
years of living together, she had got a new job with 12-hour
days and a new boyfriend. Since I work completely different
hours to her, we became ships in the night and the most we
interacted was a five-minute catch-up before bed, usually
with her on the loo while I was brushing my teeth. Not the
most hygienic thing, but an indication of our level of friendship. This is a cliché that has been repeated in countless
people's stories. One friend gets a boyfriend and the single
friend feels abandoned. Since it's a cliché, we all know how
it ends. Because I cared about this friendship more than any
other, I was determined not to let that be the ending. I told
my life coach about the situation and she suggested that I sit
down and talk to her about it. Logical, makes sense. And . . .
make a plan to go on a date once a month.

Whoa, no way! That's ridiculous and only something
you do with someone you are dating. That's not a normal

friendship thing. Michelle agreed, it wasn't normal. But healthy communication is also not normal and if you want better than the norm, then you have to start behaving that way. On the way home, I couldn't stop thinking about the amount of fear that was in my chest. The fear was coming from the fact that I had already decided how the conversation was going to end and I continuously pictured her laughing in my face at that suggestion. In reality though, if I couldn't ask the closest person to me for something, even if it was unconventional, then were we really that close? Surely in my closest friendship, I shouldn't feel *this* nervous about being vulnerable, but I did it. I asked for what I needed and she agreed. She didn't think it was silly, she also thought we hadn't spent enough time together and that conversation meant we both took out our diaries and found an evening where we were both free and committed to actually going outside our flat and doing something fun together.

This is not an idea that I would have come up with by myself and my housemate would have certainly not suggested it, but it worked because I vocalized something I needed. It doesn't matter that it isn't the norm because you get to define your own relationships and if a unique set-up is required to make both parties happy, then so be it. If I had waited for her to figure out that I was missing her either via passive-aggressive comments or a blow-up, our friendship would have been more fragmented than it needed to be.

Instead of measuring someone's love based on how much they are able to predict your desires, remember that your needs change, so it is practically impossible to make assumptions. If you are guilty of the former, you aren't asking for someone to listen and understand you, you're asking for predictability, and humans are not predictable – even you! The same situation could happen twice, and depending on the time of the year or the person involved, how you would like someone to respond could change.

The solution to overcoming the vulnerability is only asking for what you need from people who have a proven track record of being there for you in the past – let yourself be vulnerable in a safe way by making sure it's a person with whom you feel comfortable being a little more emotionally exposed. Asking for what you need from a person who has never provided that for you in the past is riskier and means that your vulnerability is going to a person who doesn't deserve it and hasn't earned it.

But what happens when you ask for what you need and it isn't provided? This was the situation with a client who had recently read Gary Chapman's *The Five Love Languages*. In his book, he talks about how we all give and receive love differently, and he has a quiz on his website that allows people to discover their love language. The five are: Words of Affirmation, Acts of Service, Receiving Gifts, Quality Time, and Physical Touch. My client had discovered that her top love language was words of affirmation and when she told her partner this, he responded by saying that it didn't feel authentic to give forced compliments. I explained to my client that it shouldn't be forced – she was asking for her partner to vocalize positive thoughts about her that he might already be thinking, but not saying out loud. Of course, it wasn't going to feel authentic at first because it is not his norm or his go-to love language, but all relationships take work, platonic and romantic. Ultimately, if I told someone I was dating what I needed and a specific way they could help me feel more loved and appreciated, and they ignored that, then that is a red flag I need to be paying attention to. There are situations which will arise where your partner might not be able or want to meet your needs, but in those cases, they should be open and willing to have a conversation about it where you can feel seen and heard and you can come up with a solution that suits you both. The reason why we don't ask for what we need is because it can be rejected, like my client was. That will hurt, but ignoring it and making excuses for the people in our life will only build resentment and create more hurt in the long run. It is better to face that hurt upfront and realize that the person in your life can't provide what you need. When you move on, you will have more time to find someone who can meet those needs.

Take Action: One of the things that starts to happen when you are honest and ask for what you need is that your honesty revolutionizes the relationship and allows more vulnerability to exist. Since I became clear and direct with the people in my life, and stopped all the guesswork, that vulnerability has grown to the point where I can ask them anything, and I know I will get an honest response, shared in the most compassionate way possible. You are going to need a person in your life like that for this exercise. It has to really be someone you trust fully with vulnerable information because otherwise, this exercise will go sideways and end in hurt feelings. Once you've found that person, I want you to ask them the following questions:

- What is one thing I could do in my life that would dramatically improve it?
- What boundaries can I set that would dramatically improve my life?
- Which person can I set boundaries with to dramatically improve my life?

Sometimes we are too close to the source to see the areas of our life that need work. Asking one of my friends these questions was actually what motivated me to set boundaries, because for the first time I realized that other people saw my lack of boundaries as well.

CHAPTER 4:

SETTING BOUNDARIES IN DIFFERENT CONTEXTS

As Per My Previous Email: Boundaries in the Workplace

Being a workaholic is easier than it's ever been. Now that we have technology, there is an unspoken expectation for us to constantly be contactable and available. If you lack self-love, work becomes the most accessible tool to fill the voids where self-esteem should be. And in a society where being busy is glorified, it's not a vice that society easily sees as unhealthy. If you are unable to boundary your work – whether that's working more hours to impress your superiors or not being adequately compensated for your time and energy – it is extremely fragile to base your self-worth on your productiveness. If you don't have boundaries in your work life, it inevitably will have an impact on other areas of your life. For example, if you are constantly typing emails on your phone when people are trying to spend time with you, or you are interrupting conversations to pick up the phone every time it rings, it's going to make your relationships harder. Someone being on the phone in front of me is one of my boundaries and I don't tolerate it. If you are going to spend the whole dinner working, then we might as well not be having dinner. If the majority of workaholics were honest with themselves, the workplace provides the feelings they crave of being needed, and it makes them feel important. The urgent requests aren't actually as urgent as they perceive them to be in their brain, but instead they love how that busyness distracts them.

Boundaries are difficult to lay down in all settings, but within the workplace, the fear of being demoted or fired is often used to validate a general fear of standing up for ourselves, and it's therefore used as an excuse. Using this fear, we set up a false dichotomy between speaking our minds and losing our jobs, or swallowing our protestations and having to live with the continued resentment as we suffer in silence. There is a middle ground between those two choices.

The way we flip this mindset is two-fold. First of all, it is important to understand that just because someone likes you, doesn't mean they respect you. Of course, your superior loves the fact that you are often the last one in the office and that they are never pressured to give you a pay rise. It benefits the company that they can take advantage of this and they will continue to take advantage until you put your foot down. Obviously, there are situations where overtime and working to prove yourself is necessary, but you must be honest with yourself. Ask yourself if that is the exchange going on here, or whether it's being driven out of insecurity. The second part of the mindset shift is realizing your time and energy is worth something. The way worth is measured in our society is monetarily, and the best way to have your time and energy appreciated in your job is financial compensation. If you believe your time and energy belongs to others or lacks importance, then that will be shown in the way you operate in the workplace.

As well as knowing your worth when it comes to compensation, it is also important to have strong boundaries around money. Every job involves elements of working for free or doing things for exposure or networking, but knowing where your boundaries are limits how much time and energy is being spent without being appropriately compensated. For me, I don't do unpaid work unless the opportunity benefits me, and the criteria that determine that shifts from job to job. In my industry in particular, a lot of companies like to guilt you into accepting a job with no payment because it's an important issue. I often get emails that suggest that if I care about mental health, I should accept that there is no budget and do the work anyway. I object to that. Of course I care about mental health, but if that became my rule, then I would never get paid because every single job I do relates to mental health. Unscrupulous companies may manipulate a person's passion for a cause or love for their job to avoid paying them what they are worth. My boundaries are now very firm in this area. If a brand doesn't see that my time, energy and qualifications are worth money, then it shows that they don't really value my knowledge and content. I also believe it's about respect. If these companies were honest, the excuse of not having the budget for my work is simply down to lack of planning. If you can pay for the venue, the catering and the employees of your company, you can also pay for the speaker at your event.

Healthy work communication

A necessary part of good boundaries is clear communication. If you expect others to communicate well with you, then you need to extend the same courtesy. Good communication not only includes a prompt response time, but also a respect for other people's time and good listening skills. This is important in both the small and big things. For example, if you are a poet looking for an agent and on their submission page, it says "no poetry", do not waste someone's time. It implies you believe you know better than them. Some would view it as shooting your shot. I see it as bad boundaries. An example of good boundaries is texting before you call to ask if a person is free and another is responding to emails, even if it is just to decline their request. If you are unable to respond to the queries in the email, an acknowledgement of their email is often appreciated. If the content of the email requires time for the work to be completed, it is good practice to respond with a date when they can expect a reply. An example of this would be: "Thank you so much for sending along your content. I will take a look at it over the week and get back to you by the end of next week with necessary changes."

If someone contacts you on a personal email address or your personal phone number, then you are allowed to set boundaries and communicate that: "Thanks for getting in touch. This is actually my personal number. I have seen your email and I will get back to you when I am back in the office on Monday. Have a great weekend!"

Out-of-hours boundaries

There was a time when you could clock off from work the moment you left the office, but thanks to technology, most people never truly switch off. Not only is this not healthy, but it isn't productive to constantly be on call, and in the long term it will lead to you being burnt out. I found myself in this position at the end of 2019. I get constant urgent social-media requests on weekends, in the evenings and sometimes as late as midnight. So at the beginning of 2020, I made it a priority to set some stronger work boundaries. What I realized is that while these requests were being framed as urgent, the majority weren't, so I started using two phrases more.

"This is not urgent or important."

I would rarely use this phrase to another person, but I would say to myself to remind myself to evaluate how much

I really needed to respond in this instant, or whether they could wait until the next workday morning.

"A lack of planning on your part does not constitute an emergency on my part."

Again, I rarely say this to another person verbatim but will reword it in an email mentioning how long they have taken: "Since I have not heard from you in the last month, I will be unable to provide you the content by tomorrow but you will receive it next week". Within my industry, there is a strong double standard that when they want their content, they want it now, even if it's less than 24 hours notice. Except when I send the content across, it is common that I won't hear back from anywhere between two weeks to over a month and yet, when they finally respond, again it will be an emergency so when I respond in this way, it is highlighting this double standard and the difference in time expectations.

Using both these phrases, and also learning to turn my phone on airplane mode, made a massive difference in my life. Not only did I truly start noticing how much I was constantly working, but also how often I was accepting that a task was urgent because they said it was, rather than evaluating it and deciding for myself if it was urgent. Depending on your job, there will be different levels of feasibility, but make sure you are being honest with yourself. Even if you are not able to decline outright, you can still boundary your time off. For example, let's say you get a call out of hours but don't feel fully comfortable not picking up at all. Instead, you can answer, but boundary the time that is spent on the call. Usually, when someone calls at an inconvenient time, they know it and will often start the call with something like "Hey! Is now a good time?", at which point you can easily say, "Yes, now works. I have 15 minutes." Even if they don't say that, I will often pick up the phone and say something like, "Hey! Just a heads-up, I have another meeting in 15 minutes." It is important when you set out-of-hours boundaries that you define them in a way that suits you. A reminder: they are your boundaries and you can change them when you like.

For me, I now have a boundary that I don't reply to work emails or texts out of hours, with the only exception being my agents. This means that even if others have bad work boundaries, because my boundaries are firm, their out-of-hours requests do not affect me. In addition, when I reply in the morning or on Monday, I purposely never apologize for the delay because I do not want to set the expectation that contacting me warrants an immediate response. These are my boundaries, and yours might differ depending on your industry, but for me, I am lenient if the request is a one-off or it is a singular emergency requiring my urgent attention. What I do not want to set a precedent for is that this type of out-of-hours communication is acceptable in all situations. One of the best ways to communicate these boundaries is not responding – just because someone calls doesn't mean you have to answer. This principle works for all forms of communication. A received email doesn't require an instant reply. Just because your boss has poor boundaries outside of office hours doesn't mean your boundaries have to be just as weak. If this continues to be the case where you are working late into the evening or on weekends, you are also allowed to ask for compensation for that. Here are two options for starting a discussion:

"I have found in the last year that I have worked more weekends than I haven't. I was not made aware of this when I was hired, and while I understand it is necessary, it would be great if one afternoon a week, I could pick up my kids from school in lieu of those extra hours I am working."

"I understand the reduction in staff has meant that my workload has increased, and I was wondering if this could be spread out more evenly among the team so my working hours don't extend into every evening. If this is not possible, it would be great if this could be taken into consideration when salaries are readjusted at the end of the year."

Saying no in a professional way

You are allowed to place limits on what you are capable of doing within a work day. Your limits do not have to match other people's in the workplace and you are allowed to decide what is too much for you and what is an absolute no.

For me, my hard limit is I don't do any content in my underwear. Some people don't understand this boundary because I have done photo shoots in bikinis, but other people don't need to understand your boundaries. What's curious is that people I work with are never the people who question why. I told my social-media agent once in our first meeting and he has never asked why; I don't even hear about the jobs that involve underwear because he declines them automatically. On one job, however, I found myself bending on this boundary and I wish I hadn't. In my multi-hyphenate job, sometimes I am hired as a life coach and sometimes I am hired as an influencer who is most known for my viral campaign around scars. I am also sometimes hired as an author or as a speaker. While these obviously overlap and there are some jobs for which I am hired in all of those capacities, on this one job I was doing, I had been clearly hired as a life coach for a life-coaching session that was going to be recorded for TV.

They asked me on the day if I could show the scars that are on my stomach, but because I had not been given notice of that, I was wearing a dress. If they had told me before, I would have no issue with lifting my top slightly to show the scars and worn jeans so that it would be easy to access my scars but since I hadn't, it meant there was now footage of me in my underwear. It was only after I filmed my content, that the person I was filming with was asked the same thing, at which point she turned around and went "No, I won't be doing that," and my first thought was, "Why didn't I say that?" There were a number of reasons why I felt more pressured than she did, but her setting her boundaries made me realize that I should have reiterated mine. Since it is never too late to set a boundary, after the shoot, I emailed my agent to make sure no footage of me in my underwear was used. He called me.

"Why didn't you just say no?" It was a good question.

"I know, I know. There won't be a next time."

And that's the best you can do when you bend your own boundaries – learn from them and next time, don't make the same mistake. The reason why I didn't say no is the same reason a lot of people don't say no in the workplace: the pressure of other people and thinking whatever is being asked of you is a normal request that someone else would say yes to. But you don't need to conform to the norm, whether that's working extra hours or performing additional tasks that aren't part of your job description.

Another issue that people struggle with when saying no is how to communicate that when new tasks are being given to them. It is worse to take on too many tasks and have people waiting on you than it is to admit when your workload is too heavy, and ask for assistance so that the work can get completed on time. This is the same if a task slowly changes over time. I found myself in this position last year when I agreed to help organize a speaking panel for five authors. I hadn't heard any information for a month and when I next heard back, the event had changed to include 10 people and was a much larger production than I had agreed to. I knew I couldn't commit to that extra workload and event organization was not one of my strengths, so I communicated that. They completely understood, but because the profits were going to be split evenly, they asked if I could take a lower share. I agreed to that and allowed them to decide what amount would be fair. I know if I had pushed myself to do something that I am not very good at doing, I would have not only been stressed, but also performed the rest of the work I needed to do at a lower quality (like writing the proposal for this book!). In the moment, you might feel like you are not pulling your weight, but in most cases, people would rather you let them know so that the work still gets done, than have you struggle through it and either deliver it late or underdeliver. In this instance, I gave them my reasons because they were friends of mine. But over the last few years, I have stopped giving a reason as to why I am unable to do something or attend an event and here are a few ways to communicate that:

- Thanks for considering me. Unfortunately, I am unable to make that work.
- Thanks for your email, unfortunately that doesn't sound right for me but _____ might be a better fit?

- Thanks for the invite. Sadly, I will be unable to attend. Good luck with your event!
- I don't have the time to commit to new projects at the moment, but really appreciate you thinking of me.

There will be times and situations when you will want to work the long hours or go the extra mile to prove yourself, but in those moments, question why you are truly doing it. Are you doing it because you are seeking approval or because you have the perception that this specific project will contribute to a promotion? Get clear on this to avoid disappointment and unmet expectations. As a result, you won't feel resentment for the extra work because it won't feel like a boundary violation, but like a conscious decision you made.

Personal and professional boundaries with colleagues

When you are spending all day with people, it is normal and natural for personal relationships to form. However, there should still be a distinction between when you are colleagues or friends. For example, personal information that is shared after a few drinks should not be brought into the workplace. This does not mean your workplace relationships have to always be formal or work-related but that there should be a level of separation that is understood between you, whether directly or indirectly communicated.

Within my job, I also have people I work with who, over time, have become my friends. For the first few years of being a life coach, I worked completely alone. That was also the case when my writing and social media became part of my job but now, due both to my books and social media, I have two agents whom I also consider my friends. When you initially start learning about boundaries, it might seem really official and formal. As you get into the swing of things, you will realize that boundaries can be set in a much more casual way and as a natural part of conversations. This is what happened with both my agents.

With my literary agent, Hayley, we text when we are communicating as friends and we email when she is talking to me as my agent. If we go out for drinks, we have a strict rule against work conversations. While these rules aren't official and if I were to send a text about something work-related, there would be no issue, but it does help to keep the distinction clear. With every relationship, different boundaries work for different people. Those boundaries, for example, would not work with my social-media agent, Jamie. My social-media work is too all-consuming, and a high volume of work comes in at all hours, so it's often easier on both of our parts to text. Instead of delineating the two sides of our relationship with one communication form or another, we both often preface sentences with "as your friend" or "as your agent/client" and sometimes "as both your agent/client and friend". This extends into other areas as well. For example, if I were to contact Jamie as a friend outside of working hours, I wouldn't apologize, but if I contacted him out of working hours about a job, I would both acknowledge that and apologize.

When this line gets blurred, this is when conflicts in the workplace start to happen. For example, if you were to disclose to a colleague privately that your mental health was not in a great place and then they took that as an indication you couldn't do your job properly or started to doubt your competency, that would not only be hurtful personally but disrespectful professionally. Similarly, let's say you were dissatisfied with a colleague's work and communicated that. If they brought that up at the weekend while you were hanging out, that would seem out of place. We need to allow people to have their work self and their private self.

When personal and professional boundaries get blurred in an office setting, the group dynamic can often create a toxic office culture. You are allowed to opt out of office drama or gossip. Voicing your discontent the moment it is brought up might seem scary, but allows for healthier communication. An integral part of healthy communication is asking the person to talk to the person that they have an issue with. That is the only person who can solve it – talking to other colleagues will not only escalate the drama but also detracts from your ability to focus on your work.

"Talk to them about it. Maybe they aren't aware they are doing it," is an easy, non-confrontational way to not get involved. If they continue the conversation, I would simply say, "I'm sorry it is annoying you, but I can't help you with the situation. You need to talk to them directly."

Setting boundaries with a boss

Of course, setting boundaries with an authority figure when there is a power dynamic in play complicates things, but remember that boundaries lead to increased respect.

In one of my previous jobs, I worked in a hospital ward. Prior to being allowed on the ward, there was a probation period where you had to show patients where they needed to go. This probation period was meant to help you learn your own way around the hospital and assist with interacting with patients for the first time. In the middle of the probation period, my shifts had been changed and I found myself with a new supervisor. Despite the fact I had been doing these shifts for over a month, this new supervisor wanted to send me on a "treasure hunt" to see if I knew how to direct patients to the right location. This treasure hunt included different places in the hospital, and I was to report back once I had located all of them. I did as she asked and when I reported back, she then decided I hadn't learned enough, so sent me on another "treasure hunt". The third time this happened, I calmly explained that while I understood the purpose of these treasure hunts, every time I went off on one, I was unable to help patients. That was the true purpose of my job and I didn't feel this treasure hunting was a useful way to utilize my time. She told me that I was of no use to patients if I didn't know where everything was. I told her that there was a reason I had a map in my hands and I was perfectly equipped to use that map if needed. She then proceeded to ask me if I had actually completed the last treasure hunt and if so, to tell her the code for the prayer room.

"I went to the door, I didn't go in," I said.

"See, you are lying! You would know the code if you had actually done what I told you to," she responded.

"No, I went only to the door because I didn't think it was appropriate to walk into a prayer room, where people are praying for their ill loved ones, for a treasure hunt."

At this point, she turned to one of my older colleagues standing next to her and said, "Youngsters these days have no respect. I'm reporting you to the head office."

The following week, when I was asked to go to the head office on my shift, I was told that they had heard about the events from the previous week and while they were not going to say that my supervisor was in the wrong, they were clear in stating that I myself had not done anything wrong. They would be putting this down to a personality conflict and resolving it by expediting my probation period so I could start work on the ward immediately. A number of my colleagues expressed their jealousy and also voiced that they had had similar situations with the same woman, but were too worried about the repercussions to either stand up to her or tell anyone else about it. The reason why I was able to do so is because I knew my career values and that my most prioritized value is time. I didn't appreciate my time being wasted, but more than that, these treasure hunts were actually preventing me from doing my job. I had trained for six months to do this job and the reason I applied in the first place was because of my own personal experience of being in hospital and having 15 surgeries as a child. When I got called into head office, I told them that I wanted more than anything to move onto that ward so that I could start working with children directly, but I refused to let that come at the expense of being treated disrespectfully. Being dismissed due to my age was unacceptable considering the fact that my young age is exactly the reason why I was qualified for this job. I was only two years out of hospital myself and I had direct experience that meant I could relate to the children in the ward.

When standing up to a boss, of course there is a calculated risk that only you can determine in your particular situation. Within the communication I had with this supervisor, I remained respectful, and therefore I could stand by my words and actions when I was called into head office to explain.

Unprofessional communication

There will be the odd occasion when someone steps over the line of professionalism and becomes rude or insulting. Just because you are being paid to be there doesn't mean people can treat you or speak to you how they like. There was a job I did last year where I learnt this lesson. I had been invited to attend an event hosted by a fashion brand where there was a roundtable discussion about how we can make the fashion industry more diverse, or so I thought. When I turned up, I discovered that I wasn't in fact attending the event, but speaking at the event. Since all communication goes through my agent, I texted him to check where the miscommunication had been. He was just as shocked as I was and forwarded me the email that stated nothing about me actually speaking. I have had a policy for two years now that I do not do public speaking for free. I knew that if I followed my policy, I should not have taken part and simply stated that they were very misleading in the email but for whatever reason, I decided to stay. If I look back on it now, I would say that decision came from the fact that I knew a number of people in the room, and I worried that if I followed through on my policy, I would come across as rude and unprofessional. In fact, they were the ones being unprofessional but because my concern lay with them, I could not see that.

I told my agent I would stay, he said he was going to request a fee and I insisted that it was OK and that it would "look bad to ask now". Turns out I would immediately regret it the moment the company boasted they had made £2.3 million in their first year. So they could make that amount, but not pay their speakers? Throughout the event, I spoke out about the lack of diversity in the industry especially in regards to race, as I was one of the only two people who were people of colour. When it was time to take a break, the husband of the CEO came up to me and said, "Wow! You must be fun at parties," presumably a dig at the fact that I had been one of the more vocal people in the room. My job that day was not to appease him, and having been actively campaigning for more racial inclusion in the fashion industry, I had been accustomed to the negative reactions I received, so tried to deescalate the situation by joking that he should see me once I have a glass of wine. The event continued and after a few more passing comments about how I should "lighten up" and "not everything needs to be so serious", I was glad to be out of that room. Upon leaving the room, I called my agent and voiced my annoyance. He suggested that he email a complaint to the PR team but I insisted that it wasn't a big deal and just the average bullshit you have to deal with when it comes to the patriarchy.

However, there was an after-party and I had committed prior to these comments that I would show up and because I stick to my word, I turned up. Within 10 minutes of arriving, a friend and I were laughing together and walked past this same man, at which point he declared, "Oh look, she can smile!" While it had all been said in jest, there was definitely an undertone to it that made me uncomfortable. In a normal situation, I would have approached him directly, but as I was being hired by the CEO and not her husband, I decided to just flag it with the CEO herself. I didn't need anything to be done but I thought it should be brought to her attention. When saying goodbye, I simply stated that her husband had made a few comments about me being "too intense", and jokes about me needing to smile and lighten up; I said that these comments did not match the feminist branding of her company, and that if you invite someone to voice their opinions, they should not have to endure passive-aggressive comments for doing just that. She apologized and I went to get my coat. As I went to the door, he approached me again.

"Hey! My wife said that you had an issue with me and I apologize if you felt that way but I just think you have some anger management issues."

I stood there in shock. I didn't even respond. If I had responded in the moment, it wouldn't have been words that I would have been proud of, so I turned around and left with my friend.

The next morning I sent the following text to my agent:

"Hey! I changed my mind about yesterday's event. I went to the after-party for a bit and at the end, the husband of the CEO, who had been in the room all day and works for the company, came up to me and said he thinks I need anger management. It's one of the most unprofessional things that has ever been said to me and unless I am raising my voice or you are my therapist, you have no right to say something like that. The fact they didn't pay me and I spent my entire day with them voicing my opinion, only for it to be twisted into an 'angry feminist' is disgusting. I never once raised my voice or made it personal about anyone in the room. I disagreed with her husband on a few points and voiced that and I understand I have a particularly direct and passionate way of speaking but I was in no way angry. I find it totally unacceptable and from the get-go, they were sneaky in the way of going about this in lying about which companies were attending and lying about the format of the event. I have gone over the initial DM and not a single brand that was mentioned was in attendance. I don't know the best way to go about this but at the very least, I want to make it known how unacceptable that comment was. Xx"

You can always set a boundary later. This is a unique situation where the boundary was set not only via my agent but the event organizer's PR agency, who would then eventually forward it directly to them. Upon receiving the email, the PR representative apologized profusely and said, having been in the room all day, that I had not been aggressive once and they had been really pleased with all the comments I had made and loved how passionate I was. They said they would pass this onto the CEO and told me that there was footage from the whole day and that the conversation had been recorded. They had since gone through the footage and not once in the event did I raise my voice or get angry. I received an apology later on that day from the CEO who offered to go for lunch to "settle this", but as with most of the boundaries I set, I had said what I wanted to say. The lunch would not have been for me, and would not have made me feel better but instead would be for her to ease over her own discomfort and probably ensure that this situation wasn't talked about publicly online.

In this situation, I chose to never work with this company again. Depending on your own situation, you might choose to either never work with the individual or leave the company in its entirety, but money is never a reason you should have to tolerate abuse, gaslighting or insulting behaviour. I acknowledge that it requires financial privilege to be able to leave a job because of this, but staying in the situation will also come at a risk of your mental health. Especially since most jobs are all-consuming, spending that many hours in a toxic climate will not only affect your self-esteem but also your general perception of yourself.

Take Action: Most smartphones have features now to either limit screen time or have a cut-off time. Start using your out-of-office feature. Take a look at the notifications you are getting on your phone and decide which ones would help you switch off. Could you limit your email notifications after a certain time or could you put your phone on silent once you leave the office? Since the majority of jobs involve some element of technology, managing this better could help you have better downtime. If you worry that you could miss something urgent, smartphones also allow you to make exceptions for certain contacts, so you can mute all phone calls except for those from your boss, for example.

Don't Speak to Me Like That: Boundaries in Romantic Relationships

Romantic relationships function best when we know where we end and another person begins and we are able to respect each other's boundaries. Having boundaries within a romantic relationship means respecting that each partner has their own views, and allowing those separate opinions to exist without needing to force them to match. It's the maintenance of separate schedules and respecting that each individual will have different priorities. Most people get on board with these ideas. But when I discuss the fact that boundaries in romantic relationships also mean taking responsibility for your own emotional well-being, I often get pushback. For example, it is not your partner's job to make you feel beautiful. In most relationships portrayed in the media, we have normalized making your romantic partner your top priority, having expectations that your partner can fulfil the needs you are unable to meet yourself and any insecurity you have can be healed by having a partner. I take a different point of view. How can a partner make you happy if you don't even know what makes you happy? How can you expect your partner to make sure you feel loved, if you are not making yourself feel loved? We cannot look to other people to heal the wounds that exist inside us. When we ensure that our own needs are being met and we fulfil our own requirements, it places fewer expectations on other people to do a job that we should be doing for ourselves.

The healthiest relationships occur when each party is responsible for their own self-esteem and the maintenance of their mental health. Of course, partners are there to support you, but ultimately, it is your responsibility. Being less reliant on a partner doesn't mean the love will be diminished, it simply means you want them around rather than need them around. The difference between want and need is liberating because it means you have chosen a partner, not kept them around for necessity. We have romanticized needing another human, when I believe the most romantic thing is *not* needing someone but wanting them around anyway. In fact, needing someone is a quick way to remove any romance in a relationship. Love works best when it is freely given, and starved when it comes loaded with expectations.

How early is too early?

In the first stages of a relationship or even in the dating stage, people avoid setting boundaries because they believe it is too early on in the relationship. Some people believe it's too serious and some worry you can't ask that much too soon. Others have the illusion that conversations about communication are only reserved for those in a committed relationship. All of these ideas are flawed. Boundaries, and learning how to set them, are about setting the standard of how you want to be treated. You set a precedent in a new relationship for the standard you expect. In fact, it's harder to ask for a change in behaviour after you've set a precedent for accepting that behaviour. Instead of adjusting your standard to what the person is willing to give you, you need to make the decision, hold firm on that standard and if that person cannot meet your expectations, find a new person who will.

The first time I set a boundary in the early stages of dating, it felt strange and unnatural. We were a month into dating and he had an issue with his family that meant he might have to cancel our plans. I understood, but told him to let me know by midday if he was free or not so I could make other plans. I didn't hear from him until 9pm, when our date was meant to be at 7pm. When he messaged, I told him that it wasn't OK and that I would have much rather he cancelled and rearranged even if he had ended up being free. It quickly turned into a heated conversation in which he accused me of overreacting because I had received rejections for a book manuscript that day, and then told me to go to bed and he would speak to me in the morning. There were a million things wrong with this communication, as is often the way when setting boundaries the first time in a new context, but I think the thing that bothered me most was the instruction to go to bed as if I were a child. Regardless, we stopped for the night because our conversation had become unproductive, and the following day he texted me as if nothing had happened. I asked him if we were going to talk about yesterday and he replied asking if I wanted to talk about my book. I told him that no, I was fine about my rejections but I wanted to talk about our fight. There was a large part of me that wanted to go along with his plan to pretend nothing had happened, but part of my journey in discovering boundaries was choosing the more uncomfortable option. I told him that I was capable of separating my feelings about my book rejections from my feelings about him not letting me know, and that communication in general was really important to me. The conversation was a long (and very messy!) one, but when we had resolved everything, I felt proud of myself that I had vocalized what I needed.

In the moments when I doubted myself and wondered whether I was making a big deal out of nothing, I asked myself if I wanted to date someone who doesn't have the decency to cancel. It was less about the cancelling, and more about the fact that the conversation itself was the most illuminating way to find out I was in the wrong relationship. It showed me that he couldn't apologize, didn't take accountability and would rather pretend it didn't happen than have the hard conversations. All of those things were turn-offs, as my highest value in relationships is good communication. Setting those boundaries allowed for me to see that he wasn't the person for me.

The reason why I believe in setting boundaries from the outset is because if this is how they behave in the beginning while they are still trying to impress you, then that behaviour is only going to get worse the further you get down the line. The more I got used to validating my own needs and realizing they are of importance, the less the doubts were able to creep in. That voice that told me I was "making a big deal out of nothing" became easy to ignore when I realized it wasn't my voice. It was the voice of my ex, who had been skilled at gaslighting my feelings and needs. Continuing to ask for more and to raise the standard of people I date has only delivered healthier communication and simpler relationships – so even if you have those doubts, rest assured that the rewards that are waiting for you are worth getting to on the other side.

Can I still set boundaries if it's a casual relationship?

Yes, even if you are just sleeping together, you are allowed to set boundaries. If you are scared to set boundaries with a person you are sleeping with, that isn't a person you should be sleeping with. The person you are most scared to set a boundary with is the person you need to set boundaries with the most. At their core, boundaries are about how you want to be treated; the seriousness of a relationship shouldn't determine the respect you receive. If a person doesn't listen when you say no, shames you or tries to persuade you when you feel unsure about a certain sexual position, those are boundary violations. The boundaries you set don't have to be limited to the bedroom simply because your relationship is. In a casual relationship, you have fewer expectations of the other person, but at a minimum you should have trust and respect.

For me, even in casual relationships, I need the other person to respect my time and stick to the plans we make. Especially with the introduction of dating apps, changing timing and cancelling last minute has become so normalized that I often find myself having to set this boundary. In one instance, I was making plans with a guy to come around the next day when he replied saying he was unsure and he would let me know tomorrow. This wasn't going to work for me, even in a casual relationship. I don't like being treated like an option that you can cancel if a better offer comes along, so I told him so.

> "That's not how this works. Let me know now if you are free, and if not, I'm making other plans."

I got an instant response.

> "Alright, Miss Sassy. 3 p.m. it is."

It amused me that someone who was so unsure of his schedule for tomorrow could reply so instantly and specifically. His schedule didn't change, but his respect for me did. The "Alright, Miss Sassy" was a silly ego move to try to regain some element of control back, but the rise in respect was indicated by the rise in his priorities. Similarly, last-minute dates are a no-go for me as well. If I get a last-minute text, especially late at night, my reply is, "Thanks for the offer!

I'm going to need more notice if you want to spend time with me, though."

There was a time in my life when I would have worried so much about how I was perceived and so wanted to be seen as "carefree" that I would have accepted his original offer to wait until tomorrow, only to be disappointed if he cancelled. Setting boundaries avoided that by demanding that my time be treated with respect. Don't accept what you are given – ask for what you want.

Being perceived as needy or naggy

Early on in romantic relationships, people want to come across as the best version of themselves. Whilst this can be an issue in all romantic relationships, it is more common when the relationship is between a man and a woman for the woman to end up performing the "easy-going, low maintenance" ideal that straight men love to advertise for on their dating profiles. I say performing because it's not real or even realistic. When I see "easy-going" or "low maintenance", I hear a man wanting a partner with no needs, who will expect nothing of him and most of all, will not start any drama (i.e. not have conversations around communication). If that's the kind of partner you want to attract, the one who will tell you that you are making a big deal out of nothing every time you set boundaries or ask for your needs to be met, carry on presenting yourself as easy-going. Otherwise, set boundaries from the outset.

These words seem to only be weaponized against women. "Needy" makes women doubt whether they should have needs and "naggy" makes women doubt whether they should vocalize them. As a result, only women are taught to question whether they are asking for too much or whether their needs are valid. Everyone's needs are valid. It's the same with your emotions. However you feel is how you feel and don't ever let anyone make you feel like your feelings are not legitimate. Part of becoming more boundaried (and selfish!) is recognizing that whatever your needs are, they are important and deserve to be fulfilled – even if another person needs less, even if an ex-partner told you that you were crazy for asking for more. Every human has different needs: some need more communication than others, others need more reassurance, and some need more space. It's not a competition for whose needs are valid and whose needs are crazy, it's a process to find whose needs match your own. The key is not to change your needs but instead to find someone who is capable of fulfilling them. Lower your standards and you will lower your self-respect and self-worth. You can't ask too much from someone who is equipped to fulfil your needs.

Addressing the fear of being single

One of the main reasons people do not set boundaries in romantic relationships is because they fear losing the person. You are allowed to have fear setting a boundary, but that is not a valid reason not to set it. Be scared while setting the boundary. If a boundary is the reason why someone leaves you, that is not a person you want to be with. There is a quote I love from the film *Frozen 2,* when Anna apologizes and Kristoff says, "It's OK, my love is not fragile." In good relationships, love is not fragile enough to disappear because you set a boundary. If you fear that a boundary is going to make people stop loving you, you likely had a childhood where love was taken away as punishment and given as a reward. In healthy relationships, love should not be used in this way.

This is why it's imperative to have cemented in your mind that being single is better than being in a bad relationship. We all date shitty people. It says nothing about you if you attract someone who treats you badly, but the difference between a person with boundaries and one without is that the former gets rid of the shitty person faster. A person with boundaries knows that if the person in front of you cannot meet your needs and requirements, then another person exists who will. We need to lose this scarcity mindset that there is only one person who can fulfil our requirements.

If you hold on to the belief that there is more than one person out there for you, your energy around dating shifts when setting boundaries. The difference between "I need you to fulfil this need" and "'I have this need, can you fulfil it?" is that the person asking the latter doesn't care about the outcome. The former implies that you are relying on that one individual to fulfil your needs, while the latter implies that your needs exist and you are seeing if the other person is a good match. The only way you can do that is by expressing your needs and communicating when your boundaries are being crossed. And yes, setting boundaries might make it more likely for you to lose the person you are with, but it will only ever make you lose the wrong person, in which case, you are closer to finding the right person.

Losing yourself in the relationship

As relationships progress, it becomes easier and easier to lose your individual identities and become more co-dependent and enmeshed. Societally, we also encourage it with phrasing like "my other half" and romanticizing couples that are inseparable. This is when couples almost inhabit one identity. Do you know those friends that bring along their partner without telling you because it is just expected that an invite for one means an invite for both of them? Their identity becomes the relationship, rather than keeping their identities as individuals.

While dropping everything for your partner has been idealized as romantic, it isn't, and is a fast way to lose yourself within the relationship. I remember a moment a friend spoke to me about his partner, who would drop everything to reply to his texts. If his boyfriend was in a meeting, he would excuse himself from the meeting to respond. One day, my friend sent me this text:

> I think one of the things I appreciate about you is that you have boundaries. So for example, if I want to brainstorm or need advice, I know that if you are busy or tired, you will tell me instead of dropping everything. My boyfriend drops everything for me, he'll text me in traffic or leave meetings, and it prevents me from going to him in fear he's busy or that I'm causing inconvenience and he just isn't telling me. With you, I don't feel that way because I know you will set that boundary. So in a twisted way, not dropping everything is more considerate.

This text sums up exactly why being more selfish in a relationship actually serves the relationship in the long term. We have to see ourselves as two separate individuals. We need to act like a team while also maintaining our own autonomy. When this doesn't happen, it can cause issues. A common example is the friend who shares your personal information with their partner because they "have no secrets". No, they have no boundaries. I had this happen with a friend when I shared some private information with her, only for her boyfriend to blurt it out in the middle of a party. I pulled my friend aside and asked why he knew that information. She insisted that they share everything with each other – but it was not her information to share and it was certainly not his information to publicize. In situations like this, the couple has confused privacy and honesty. They have felt that in order to have an honest relationship, all information has to be shared, almost like a public hive mind, but this breaks the trust and confidentiality in friendships. What you tell a friend should not be automatically mutual information. You have chosen to share that with your friend, not their partner, and that should be respected. In order to have these boundaries, people need to be able to separate themselves from their partners.

A lot of the same fights actually exist because people are unable to do this. A common fight I see in relationships centres around lateness and punctuality. One partner will like being on time and the other partner is always late. It often ends in the person who likes being on time being annoyed or resentful of their partner, but this is only because they see themselves as one item. There may be the occasional empty threat that you will leave without them, but both people know the threat is empty. If you are able to remember that you are separate entities, then you are able to set a boundary: tell them the time you are leaving and if your partner is not ready, say you are leaving now and they can meet you there. If it annoys your partner to arrive separately, then they can make it a priority to be ready at the right time, but their lack of punctuality doesn't need to be a reflection on you. The rare occasion

I have seen this enforced is usually done out of anger as a last resort. Last resorts aren't boundaries. Instead of seeing it as a punishment, see it as acknowledgement that you are both responsible for yourselves as individuals and as such, you can make individual decisions. Being able to separate yourselves and having boundaries to understand that your partner is not your responsibility is what allows this.

How to fight

While knowing how to settle disagreements is something that can be used in all relationships, not just romantic ones, there is often a certain type of intensity that comes with romantic relationships, especially long-term ones, because a person knows you so intimately that they know exactly what buttons to push to elicit a reaction. It is similar to the kind of closeness in families. In the book *Crucial Conversations* by Kerry Patterson, Joseph Grenny, Ron McMillan and Al Switzler, the authors state that people fall into three categories in a disagreement: those who digress into threats and name-calling, those who revert to silent fuming, and those who speak openly, honestly and effectively.

The first category of threats and name-calling can be easily boundaried by telling your partner to not speak to you like that. The same can be done if the person yells or raises their voice. If you have respect for someone, you speak to them with respect. If they cannot speak calmly, allow time to process their emotions before initiating a conversation about the issue. If they persist in calling you names, then set a consequence that if they call you names again, you will walk out of the room and they can come speak to you when they are done being hurtful. Hurtful words have no place in any conversation and disagreements should never be about who can create the most hurt.

We need to remove the idea that anyone wins or loses an argument. It's not you against your partner, it's you and your partner against the issue at hand. Seeing you both as a team working together to fix a problem flips the mentality quickly. If you have a habit of turning against each other with hurtful words, taking a deep breath together and saying, "I want us to just remember that we are on the same team and I love you and I want to resolve this" does wonders to refocus the conversation. Stop seeing the person you are setting boundaries with as the problem. You might say, "But if they didn't act that way, I wouldn't need to set the boundary," and I could easily counter, "If you set boundaries, they wouldn't behave that way". Focus on reaching the goal you both want and see the communication as teamwork.

Then there are people who prefer the silent, fuming method. The silent treatment is passive-aggressive. There is a wonderful quote in the book *Fat! So?* by Marilyn Wann that says, "Staying silent would mean that I agree to being mistreated ... And I most definitely don't agree to that." When someone says something hurtful and we "swallow it" or "push it down", those are not metaphorical phrases, they are literal. We chose to keep that feeling within us and therefore how it seeps out is in passive-aggression. It is an outlet for the resentment that builds up when boundaries have been crossed and that person has not expressed it. Unfortunately, passive-aggression and the silent treatment often make it worse because usually one party doesn't know what they have done and the other party doesn't want to tell them because "they should know". The simplest thing you can do to enhance your relationship is to stop expecting your partner to mindread. Mindreading is dependent on you having the same response every time and being so predictable that another human can guess your response. You are not a robot; humans are not predictable. Humans change and especially if you work on your personal development, your change will warrant different responses and your needs will change too.

Just because your partner can't guess what you need doesn't mean they don't want to provide that need for you. Most people want to help if you tell them how. The silent treatment breaks respect and trust. Saying, "Hey! I am not ignoring you, I just don't have the energy to talk right now" is healthier for relationships than using silence as punishment. Be vulnerable and trust in your partner enough that they will be there if you just communicate. If your partner is the one who likes to go into the silent treatment, then use this sentence:

"When we fight, I understand you need space to process but can you give me a time when we can continue the conversation? When you suddenly go silent, I worry that our relationship is over. If you told me that you needed three hours, for example, it would ease my anxiety and I would really appreciate that."

The last category of open, honest and effective communication is the ideal place to end up and having that communication in place often means you can get through any dilemma. There is a scene in the TV show *Grey's Anatomy* where a groom is being stood up at the altar. When he is asked if they should wait any longer, he responds, "If you get to the point where you are going to walk down the aisle with someone, she's earned some trust and faith. She's earned the benefit of the doubt, so I'm giving it to her. She deserves that." I don't believe in "seeing the positives" because I believe that means you overlook red flags, but I do believe in going into all conversations with a little benefit of the doubt. You are in a relationship with that person for a reason – don't assume the worst and don't play out the worst "what ifs" in your head before they have even happened.

Being able to communicate when you want to split the finances more equally or when you don't like a sex position is two sides of the same coin. You either feel safe voicing your opinion or you don't. Having the confidence to be able to communicate those issues, no matter what the context, is essential. Whenever we talk about romantic relationships, the main priority that people talk about is love. You can love a person and that love sometimes is not enough if you are completely mismatched on values. Love is not how much shit you can tolerate from someone. The way you are treated is much more important than how much you love someone. Love without respect is meaningless, and a large part of making relationships work in the long term is to figure out your communication style and how to manage disagreements.

Take Action: Whoever came up with the idea that good relationships do not take work was talking nonsense. All relationships take work because people change. To make sure you are changing together in the same direction, it is healthy to do regular check-ins where you create a safe space to be honest with each other. Some people find it best to have a weekly "marriage meeting", some prefer to do a monthly check-in and some see it like sending in your car for an MOT every year. Whatever frequency you decide as a couple, it's helpful to go through the questions together, write it down and at your next check-in, see whether you've made the changes. Some questions you could consider include:

1) Where do you feel appreciated in our relationship?
2) Where would you like to feel more appreciated?
3) Are there any boundaries we need to clarify?
4) What have you found challenging in our relationship in the last week/month/year?

---

5) Are you happy with the amount of time we spend with each other?
6) How do you feel about our sex life?
7) Do you have any concerns about our finances and how we divide costs?
8) What do I do that makes you feel loved?
9) How can I make you feel more loved over the next week/month/year?
10) Is there anything I have done or said that was hurtful since our last check-in?
11) Are there any new boundaries that we need to set?
12) Is there anything you would like to talk to me about?
13) What is something you are really enjoying about our relationship?

_____

_____

_____

_____

_____

_____

_____

_____

_____

_____

_____

_____

We Are Better Than This: Boundaries in Friendships

Boundaries within friendship are vitally important to keep the friendship healthy. In society, working on your romantic relationship is normalized, but with friendships, there is somehow this expectation that they should just work without any effort or communication issues. This is far from the case! Much like in relationships, lives change, and these changes will alter relationship dynamics in a friendship. Not every friendship will survive every transition in your life, whether that's a change in location or jobs. Also, when you start investing in your personal development, you inevitably change a lot and it isn't always easy for the other person to accept that growth.

Learning how to have boundaries is also a lesson in how to communicate. If we are going to be people with self-trust and self-worth, then we have to cut out the toxic habit of bitching. We have to stop encouraging it in our friendship group and instead encourage that person to talk to another directly. We also have to make that promise to ourselves and go directly to the person we have an issue with. Especially within female friendship groups, bonding often happens over bitching and a mutual dislike of an individual. There is actually a joke in the movie *Julie & Julia* about it, where Julie asks, "What do you think it means if you don't like your friends?" I was screaming at the screen, "YOU HAVE WEAK BOUNDARIES!" Meanwhile, her friend replies that it's completely normal and her husband responds saying that men do, which is accurate because men haven't been taught that the rest of their gender is their competition. Even though we have been taught this by others, it is our responsibility to unlearn it. My female friendships are some of the most special relationships I have in my life. They are invaluable to me and have brought so much joy and connection to my life, but that only started happening once we eliminated competitiveness, gossiping and bitchiness. We have to hold ourselves and our friendships to a higher standard than that. We are better than that and the bonds that you form over mutual dislike may be strong, but are formed on a foundation of toxicity. If that person enjoys bitching so much, then you are not excluded from the list of people they can bitch about, and if you are the person bitching, there will always be a level of distrust in your friendships.

Within my friendship group, we enacted this "no bitching" rule. When anyone started bitching, someone would step in with a simple "That's not very nice," "Go talk to her then" or sometimes we would just say, "Come on, we are better than that." It flew in the face of everything I had been taught in school about female friendships and how to bond with women – but that meant we built our friendships on a foundation of trust. It was also really comforting to be able to know that if another friend was bitching about me and I wasn't in the room, I could trust my friends to stop it and intervene, in the same way they would do if I was the one bitching. Having friendships that held me to a higher standard felt like healthy communication.

Another thing that came with healthy communication was honest friends. Prior to these relationships, I thought a friend was essentially a "yes man", who would tell you that you were right. Now I know that a "yes man" is just an echo chamber, and would give what I call "empty encouragement". If I said I wanted to go get drunk the night before an exam, they would encourage me. If I said I should stay at home to study, they would encourage me. It was all well intentioned, but no matter what I said, they would just reinforce what I already believed. When I found my own voice and set boundaries, I realized this empty encouragement boosted my ego but wasn't helpful. I wanted people in my life who wouldn't just tell me what I wanted to hear. What I discovered was true friends keep you accountable, challenge your stupid ideas, tell you when you need to apologize, and say to you, "Yes, he did bad things, but you also shouldn't have done that." Their opinions don't alter when mine did. A lot of the time, what they said wasn't what I wanted to hear, and that took some adjustment, but knowing I could rely on my friends for the truth meant I actually started to grow as a person.

An aspect that is not often discussed in relation to friendship is breakups. It's particularly strange because, in my experience, they hurt way more than any guy has ever hurt me. One of the reasons I believe this is the case is because we honour lifelong friendships and we see lost friendships as a personal failing. The shame we feel when a friendship ends becomes wrapped around being a bad person. We stay silent about it because we believe the end of that friendship is a reflection of us and that we are a bad friend.

I want to flip this idea on its head. Someone who is a "good friend" to you could be a "toxic friend" to another. The word "toxic" is used often but I believe more in "toxic dynamics" and "toxic behaviours" than "toxic people", because we are not our behaviours. We need to stop defining our "goodness" as a human on how good a friend we can be to others. There is no person who is objectively a good friend to all. The person who keeps all your secrets could be the person bitching behind another friend's back. When we keep a friend around simply because we are too scared to end it, we hold resentment against the person and inevitably, this is how bitching happens.

This journey of ending friendships and finding new and healthier ones changed my entire concept of friendship and challenged what I had always been taught about friendship. This came in three main lessons:

A friendship can end and still be a success

Ending a friendship because it is no longer working is the healthier and kinder thing to do. Keeping a friendship that is past its expiration date is more of a failure than calling it a day when it has run its course. We need to start considering that an end of a friendship doesn't mean the time spent together was a failure at all. The friendship could have been as real as you remembered it to be, and it could also be true that the friendship is no longer what it used to be. The friendship could have served you well in the past, been full of love, empathy and support, and was the perfect relationship you needed at a certain time in your life – and it can still end. No matter how long or short the friendship was, it brought value to your life. The end of that friendship does not take away the positive impact that person once had on you.

Having a go-to person for everything breaks friendships

There was a point in school I remember being really sad because I didn't have that go-to best friend that people talked about in movies. I didn't have that one ride-or-die, there-no-matter-what person to rely on and I thought that meant I was "too much", "a lot" and only "good in small doses". And then I found that person. In *Grey's Anatomy*, Meredith Grey calls Cristina Yang "my person", the one she calls when she hypothetically kills someone and needs help to bury the body. That's what my friend and I used to call each other, and we'd quote this line often. It was exactly like it was in the movies: she would turn up at my door at 3 a.m., crying, with no warning, and I would let her in. I would drop everything to be there for her, and then we both grew up and I realized adult friendships don't work like this. I realized that we were both co-dependent and it wasn't healthy.

Now, I do not believe you should have one go-to person. To rely on one human as your entire support system for your needs is a lot of pressure for that individual. Sometimes you both are going through something shit at the same time and you simply do not have the bandwidth to deal with someone else's mental health too. I am a true believer in the fact that you can't help someone else until you've helped yourself – and the flip side of that is that you can't help yourself if you are busy taking care of someone else. This also means that if you have a certain issue that would trigger one friend, you have other people to go to. No single person can help you with all your problems and can be available for every rough patch. This is why you build a support system.

As we grow into adults, our lives get busier and we lose the proximity we used to have in school and university simply because there is usually more distance, literal and figurative, between us. Partners are added to the mix and typically hold a greater importance in our lives when we are older, especially when children are in the picture. People are not going to have the emotional capacity all day every day to support you, no matter how much they love you. Friendships go through phases. Allow your friendships to fluctuate in closeness and the amount of contact that is needed.

Tests don't belong in friendships

"Stop texting first and see how many dead plants you are watering."

There are a lot of quotes about friendship that involve the idea that if you stop texting and see who notices, you can find out who your real friends are. I have seen the same in regards to social media – that if a friend doesn't support your social media posts, they don't truly support you. It's the same mentality behind any sentence that starts with, "If they loved me, they would . . ." Stop testing your friendships. You are taking an action like a lack of social-media comments to mean something it doesn't necessarily mean. Instead of embedding these hidden tests into your friendship to see whether they pass or fail, start communicating. If you want friends with good communication, that starts with you. Tell them if you miss them. Ask them what's up if they feel distant. Change "If you loved me, you should . . ." to "I know you love me, can you . . ."

This idea of testing friendships (or relationships in general) comes from a childhood where you weren't given the attention or love you needed and when you asked for what you needed, you were ignored or made fun of. So what you started doing is trying to "find out" if you are loved. As a child, you might cry loudly in your room to see if someone hears and will come in. As a teenager, you might storm out of a room mid-argument and hope someone follows you to check you are OK. Or in adulthood, you might pick a fight and see if they are willing to stick around long enough to resolve it. You were taught the wrong thing growing up. You were stuck with the same group of people as a child and a teenager so you adapted by trying to get the people who are around you to love you and actually behave in a way that aligns with that love. As an adult though, you have freedom. You get to choose new people. The problem with tests is that people don't know that they are being tested, and you start off on a principle of mistrust.

An example of this is the week when I forgot one of my best friends started her new job. It doesn't mean I don't love her, but if that is the week she decided to test our friendship, I would have failed. The only reason I didn't remember was because I was too busy thinking about me and my own problems and I only discovered that I forgot because when I called her to ask how she was, she told me about her new job. I apologized that I hadn't asked sooner and we moved on, but that wouldn't have happened if she measured my love by my memory or a single action that I didn't take. If you feel unloved or rejected by a friend not noticing something, tell them. If she was upset about it, I trust that she would have told me about it. If she was angry at me, I would have accepted that I was in the wrong and I should have remembered. A proper friend will care, apologize and do better. But we also need to take accountability and not look for signs that we are being rejected when we are not. When you assign the meaning that "they don't love me" to them not liking your social-media posts or not texting you enough, you are the one creating a meaning to hurt yourself. Instead ask for what you want and need. Trust them enough to give them a chance to deliver what you need. If they can't, then find new people.

Take Action: When you are around people who know you well and are used to you acting a certain way, it can be easy to slip into old dynamics and let your boundaries disappear. Changing relationships that already have a natural rhythm to them will take time. There is a reason why it has taken me five years to fully implement the changes in my own life. Change doesn't happen overnight and is not linear – you will slip up, you will have boundary blindspots and if you over-whelm yourself with making all these changes overnight, you will put this book away, never look at it again and not do any of the work.

Instead of looking at your growth in a linear way, under-stand that the net result will often be positive if you look at it over a greater span of time. If you looked at one week of boundary setting in isolation, it would be a rollercoaster of pass and fails, but if you looked at your growth over the next year, you will amaze yourself. When I look back at those five years, I have so many moments where I can't believe how much I have changed, and that is echoed in the sentiments of the people around me. You are setting the bar too high if you think change will be immediate. Instead of envisaging yourself as a completely different person, this week, your goal is to set 10 per cent more boundaries than you did last week. Now imagine if you did that every week for the next 10 weeks? Feels a lot more manageable now, doesn't it? And what's 10 weeks in the context of your whole life?

I Love You but I Love Me More: Boundaries With Family

Family relationships are not only how we understand love, but also the relationships through which we learn to communicate. Though you can learn effective communication and strong boundaries from your parents, you can obviously also learn the opposite. As a society, we often create rules for kids that don't apply to adults, and this creates confusion. For example, within schools, we tell children to sit down, shut up and accept what they are being taught without question. But as adults in the workplace, we want people who are confident and can express their opinions and form original thoughts. This shift is not only unnatural, but it means it creates unnecessary difficulty for children adapting to being teenagers and teenagers adapting to being adults. Teach your kids how to communicate in the way you would like them to as adults. There are no separate or different rules. If you don't want your child yelling at other adults in the workplace, then don't yell at them at home. You are never too young to learn boundaries.

Teaching these with regards to classmates in school is a useful place to start. An example of this was with my friend Jenny and her daughter Penelope. Penelope was hanging out with a girl in school who liked gossiping and because Jenny had raised her with the rule that it wasn't nice to gossip about people, she went to her mother to say how anxious it makes her feel. Jenny suggested that Penelope tell her friend that and the next day when she went into school, Penelope said to her friend, "I don't like when you gossip. If you want to be my friend, you have to stop gossiping." The next day, the friend tested the boundary and attempted to gossip again. Penelope held the boundary firm, saying, "I told you yesterday, I can't be friends with you if you keep gossiping."

When I heard that story, I was amazed. How much easier would my life have been if I had learned boundaries at 10 years old? How much easier if I had held high expectations for my friendships instead of just wanting to fit in? Penelope is growing up with strong boundaries because her mother has them. Their story is an example of how children copy what you do, not what you say. The best way to teach robust boundaries is by having them yourself and encouraging your kids to enforce their own boundaries. When you have a good relationship with yourself, you automatically have a healthier relationship with other people.

Family relationships are probably the hardest to set boundaries with, not only because they tend to be our longest relationships, but also because most people regress into old communication patterns around their family. In addition to this, as a society, we accept that family can treat us however they like "because they are family". I disagree – there are no different rules for family. I hold family members to the same standard of treatment as I would expect from any other person in my life. To change the dynamic can sometimes feel like an uphill battle. If this is your situation, then understand that you have the ability to change these generational patterns by setting boundaries. The wonderful thing is, if you bought this book, it means you are invested in your own personal growth. If you can heal the style of communication that has become the norm in your family before you have your own children, then your children won't have to heal from it in addition to you. Often, in families, we get used to the way things are, but just because it's been that way for years doesn't mean you have to accept it. As you grow as an adult, you have to understand that while your parents might be the cause of your inability to communicate, it is your responsibility to fix it.

The message that you must respect your elders and, if you are religious, "honour your father and mother" are common. Especially in traditional households and in older generations, there is less conversation about how respect should go two ways. If a child feels comfortable and safe at home, they should be able to vocalize their boundaries not only with their parents but also with their siblings and other family members. A healthy familial relationship comprises four factors:

1) **Security to feel vulnerable:** when a child feels safe to go to you with their emotions, even if it is as a result of your own words and behaviour.
2) **Safety to vocalize needs:** when a child knows their limits and what makes them uncomfortable, and feels confident vocalizing that without fear of punishment.
3) **Keeping relationships separate:** when a child knows they are only responsible for their relationships directly

with each person, and is not involved in the management of other people's relationships.

4) **Ability to apologize:** when a child receives an apology because the adult is sorry, and a parent is willing to admit when they are in the wrong.

Security to feel vulnerable

For children to flourish, they need to feel secure enough in their parent-child relationships that they are able to express their emotions and not worry that their feelings will be diminished or invalidated. This is not always done on purpose, but can occur by accident if the parents themselves are uncomfortable around emotions or simply do not have the time or energy to support the emotions that are arising. A trivial example of this is a child that is scared of a monster under their bed. How you respond to this will teach them how to navigate fear in the future. Of course, parents are humans and they don't always have time or energy to be their best selves, but go by the law of averages: if you respond compassionately 90 per cent of the time, that's what they will learn. The other 10 per cent of the time, create space to talk about it later or apologize if you responded harshly.

One of the best ways we can help our children is to get comfortable with our own emotions. If we are able to do that, we won't be quick to shut a child down when they feel the need to express theirs. If we provide this secure relationship, where a child knows that they are loved regardless of what emotions they have, it provides a safe environment in which a child can express when they are upset with you, for example. A common barrier to this is the entitlement a lot of families feel in being able to express their unsolicited opinions about your life, relationship, body and career. It is often said under the guise of love: "We are only saying this for your own good," or "If I can't tell you, who will?". While it is sometimes, but not always, well intentioned, this type of judgement is what shuts down vulnerability. Criticism is not love. Within all of us is the inherent belief that our parents are right, so while it might seem like a flippant opinion, it can affect a child's self-esteem. If you as the parent have to be right, then they are inherently wrong. When you criticize a child, they don't stop loving you, they stop loving themselves. The way you are spoken to as a child becomes your inner voice. It forms the bedrock of the belief that you are not good enough and what you do is not good enough.

Similarly, when the emotions of a family member dictate the mood of the entire family and their feelings take precedence over other family members, this means other people do not feel safe to have their emotions. If this is the case, then this needs to be boundaried because even though everyone is allowed their emotions, their emotions should not impact other people. One person's mood should never dictate the energy of a room or a home.

Safety to vocalize needs

If we want to raise children that know their own boundaries and are confident expressing their needs, then we need to foster this in childhood, no matter how inconvenient it makes it for you as parents to not have a child that obliges your requests instantly. Phrases like "because I said so" or "because I'm your mother" are examples of shutting down good communication and halting a positive questioning attitude. If they feel safe to vocalize their needs, they are given the skills to communicate if they need more space or, conversely, more attention from you. When parents want to spend every moment with their child, they prevent them from learning independence, and it is often because the parents are using their children to fulfil their own needs. On the other end of the spectrum, parents who don't spend enough time with their children end up with kids who feel neglected and that their needs aren't important. We need to meet in the middle of enmeshment and neglect and have a healthy independence between parent and child, with a respect for each other's needs.

Take the example I gave in Different Types of Boundaries (page 30) of how many times we force children to give people hugs when they don't want to. This is teaching kids that their physical boundaries don't matter. Instead, if we gave them a choice and we respected that choice, the child will know how to advocate for their bodies if someone crosses their physical boundaries in a doctor's office or a bedroom or on the street. They won't have been taught that it's polite to ignore your own needs because someone else wants to touch them when they don't want it. For this to be the case, the child needs to feel like they can vocalize their preference without fear of punishment or losing love. You may not punish them by giving them a time-out, but even if they are told they are being naughty or rude, it teaches the lesson that they shouldn't be denying physical contact they don't want.

In the same vein, showing respect for your child's privacy and belongings is crucial to start when they are at a young age, because these are lessons they take into adulthood. This respect shows them that they are allowed to be vocal when someone disrespects them or their property. A healthy parent-child relationship is one where the child feels like they can also set boundaries with their parents because boundaries work both ways.

Let's use the example of your parents continually walking into your room whenever they like. Ask them for a moment to speak to them. Saying, "Can I talk to you about something?" is an easy way to make sure they are listening. Make sure it is a good time and that you have their full attention. If they ask you what you want to talk about, but are distracted washing the dishes or doing another task at the same time, tell them you can wait until you have their full attention because this is important to you.

"When you walk into my room without knocking, I find it invasive. Sometimes I need to be alone and when I close my door, it is an indication of that. I'd really like it if you respect that. I'll make sure if you ever close your door, I knock too so that you also get alone time."

If they continue to violate your boundary, you can reinforce it by saying the following:

> "I have asked already that you knock and as that's been ignored, I'm going to start locking my door when I need privacy. I believe this will lead to a healthier relationship and I hope you understand."

The way we teach kids to have boundaries is by respecting their no. If they say "No, you cannot come into my room," respect that. If you need to talk to them, you can still continue to respect their needs while getting yours met with a simple, "OK, I won't come in, but can you come out? I need to talk to you." Too often, parents punish their children for saying no and as a consequence, we feel guilt or shame for saying no as adults. We teach them to respect other people's no by respecting theirs.

Keeping relationships separate

Families also create group dynamics, which can complicate individual relationships unless each family member is able to separate their connections. A recent example of this was a client whose parents had a bad relationship with their extended family, but my client wanted to stay in touch with his cousins and uncles. We had a number of conversations about how he was allowed to set this boundary and communicate to his parents that they do not have a right to dictate who he wants to maintain a relationship with simply because his parents have made a choice to not be in communication.

Understanding that relationships are separate outside the home is also crucial within the home. For example, making sure you keep your child out of your romantic disagreements with your partner. If this does not happen, the child can feel pressured to become their parent's confidant or therapist, and feels torn when being asked to pick a side or when they're being used as a fact-checker because one party is denying events occur. Using a child in this way is not only unfair but immoral; your child should never be the person you go to for help about relationship advice. It's essential to separate your romantic relationship out from your relationship with your child. This is also the case if you are divorced or have no romantic relationship with their other parent. This is where boundaries come in. It is not their job as a child to fix your relationship. Both parents are adults, you have a relationship separate to your child and your romantic relationship is your responsibility. Even as an adult, if your parents keep involving you in their disagreements, you can vocalize this. An example of this is:

"Hey Dad! I find it difficult when you involve me when fighting with Mum. I don't want to take a side and I don't

want your disagreements as a couple to affect my relationship with either of you, so I won't be getting involved anymore. From now on, it would be great if you could go to one
of your friends to talk about your issues with Mum and I
think it will be healthier for our relationship as well."

It is important you have this conversation with both
your parents so that neither party feels like they are to
blame. If you can, it is better to have the same conversation with both of them at the same time so they know that
the boundaries apply to both of them. Let's say the following night, there is an argument about something and your
dad accuses your mum of saying something and your mum
denies it, only for your dad to turn to you and ask, "Didn't
you hear your mother say it yesterday?", you now can opt
out of the conversation because you've set the boundary.
Here are a few options:

- "This has nothing to do with me."
- "I'm not involved in this conversation."
- "Please sort out your relationship issues yourselves."
- "They are your partner. I am not in this relationship."

Or you can just choose silence. Your dad might think that
you answering his question will give a quick solution of
who was wrong and who was right, but it actually complicates things. It creates triangulation, a theory that Murray
Bowen created in 1966 to explain that often, if a relation-

ship is in conflict, one person will involve a third party to relieve pressure.

> **Triangulation:** *an indirect communication method that uses a third party to communicate with the other party*

Fundamentally, this communication method creates a triangle dynamic that can be forged between any three members of a household, so it could be parents with a single child but it can also be three siblings or a single parent with two siblings. This becomes toxic when it's two people against one or when we use this to feel better about ourselves by pushing another person down. In coaching, we call this one-upping someone – but in order for that to take place, another person is one-down. An example of a triangle dynamic is the Karpman Drama Triangle, in which the three positions are victim, rescuer and persecutor. These are not concrete labels, but positions that people can take in an argument that shifts.

Let's say a child brings up a boundary violation to her parent and the parent starts yelling. Her other parent overhears, walks into the room and asks the child, "Why are you talking about something that happened last week? It's all in the past." The second parent has jumped into the rescuer role, pushing the child into the victim role and the first parent into the persecutor role. These roles can change, though. If the child, now feeling attacked, starts yelling and shouting abuse, they jump into the persecutor role. These roles reverse and flip around, but no one feels good because each position in this triangle dynamic feels bad. The victim feels like they can never do anything right, the persecutor is adamant they are not wrong and the rescuer just wants everyone to stop fighting, which leaves everyone feeling powerless and helpless. It doesn't solve anything and it complicates the situation, rather than focusing on the solution. Being aware of these roles and common dynamics is a way to stop your involvement in them. You can prevent the majority of triangle dynamics by keeping out of relationships that are not yours, and opting out when conversations don't involve you.

Another triangle dynamic that can happen is when a parent has clear favourites, creating the golden child and the scapegoat dynamic. One child can do no wrong and the other can't do anything right. This is a form of emotional abuse and it is not healthy for either child because both are being used to fuel a parent's self-esteem. The golden child feels pressure to maintain an unrealistic pedestal and rarely takes risks. They live with a lot of fear and internalize the message that they have to be perfect in order to be worthy. They recognize that the only reason they are held in high regard is because they are fulfilling who their parents want them to be but if they were to be themselves, that would risk falling off the pedestal and result in shame. Meanwhile, the scapegoat is vilified instead of being understood and therefore internalizes the message that they are never good enough, no matter how hard they try. They live with a lot of anger and resentment at always being seen as "different" because they do not conform to family systems. Both the golden child and the scapegoat suffer in this dynamic and in order to be liberated from it, need to understand that these labels do not define them. Understanding that this is another triangle dynamic that can be created is the best way to take your power back and realize that this is not your fault.

Ability to apologize

There are many children who have grown up in households where their parents have never apologized. It is usually in households where the adults believe that if they apologize and admit fault, then they lose power and control. Implicit in this belief is the idea that apologies demonstrate weakness. But when you apologize, in most cases, the opposite happens and your respect for the person increases. The problem with this mentality is we are not teaching children a vital life skill. We have one rule for them as children and then magically change the rules when they are adults, and expect them to know how to apologize. Instead, let's normalize making mistakes as a part of being human. Let's allow our children the idea that their parents are flawed humans who also make mistakes and that it is healthy to apologize when you need to. The child will feel respected and, in turn, will be more accountable for their actions and mistakes.

Knowing how to apologize is a skill that a lot of adults don't have because it is not something that happens enough in parent-child relationships, so if you can give your child that gift, it will serve them so well in the future. The best way to apologize according to Harriet Lerner in *Why Won't You Apologize?*, is to keep your apologies short: "Don't go on to include explanations that run the risk of undoing them. An apology isn't the only chance you ever get to address the underlying issue. The apology is the chance you get to establish the ground for future communication." We have to understand that respect is mutual and that starts with taking responsibility when you are wrong. Teaching good communication is about modelling it – if an adult were to make a mistake, you would want them to apologize so you have to echo that with children. Your child will learn that apologizing doesn't mean that you lose and that there is no shame in it.

Parents and adult children

The transition of a child turning into an adult can be a rocky one for both parties. On behalf of the parents, healthy boundaries with adult children starts with acknowledging that your child is a separate human to you. They are not an extension of you to fulfil all the dreams you never achieved and they are not your property. A lot of the time I hear parents thinking they have a right to their opinion on every part of their child's life and will freely express these opinions without being asked. This exhibits a lack of boundaries. You would never do this with another human and the moment that child left your body (or entered your life, however that happened), they became a separate human who will make decisions you don't always agree with. If they ask for your opinion, then express it. Otherwise, respect that they have the knowledge and information to make their own decisions, and if you think they are making a mistake, allow them to make those mistakes. You made your own mistakes and no matter how much you love your child, you cannot protect them from their own life lessons.

For the child, if you want to be treated like an adult, the best way to instigate the change in your dynamic is to start acting like an adult. For example, if you live with your parents as an adult or even if you go back home for the weekend, start treating their home like you were staying in a friend's parents' home. If you were at your friend's parents' house, would you offer to help take the dishes to the kitchen after a meal? You wouldn't think twice about making your bed or cleaning up after yourself because that's polite, so start creating those boundaries as a way to acknowledge that the relationship has shifted. Your parents will notice the difference, even if it isn't vocalized, and that is a good stepping stone to initiate conversations about new boundaries that need to be set in place.

Cutting family out

There are a lot of old school sayings like "blood is thicker than water" that encourage the idea that your family is the only exception to boundaries and no matter how many times they cross your boundaries, family is forever. I disagree. You don't get to choose your family, but you get to choose whether you have them in your life. Societally, this is really stigmatized, and to be estranged from any member of your family or your family as a whole is still considered taboo. It also tends to bring a lot of shame on an individual level because the person who left believes it is a reflection on them and an indication of them failing to have the relationship that is portrayed to be a given. As humans, we inherently seek the love of the people who raised us, and if they can't or don't know how to love us properly, we end up questioning our lovability. The problem with this societal message is it puts the onus on the person who is often on the receiving end of abuse, and it sends the message that the refusal to tolerate abuse is a failure.

Take the example of Meghan Markle. It has been said by many people that she was vilified by the media for cutting off communication with her father, and that she was painted to be cold-hearted, cruel and uncaring. It was felt that her father was made out to be the victim, and the media used his illness to paint him as a poor, weak man who just wanted to speak to his daughter and bent over backwards to explain why his sharing of private information to do with their relationship was normal and understandable. When your boundaries are continually being crossed, the final consequence, as with anyone else not in your family, is to have no contact and cut them out of your life. That is Meghan's right, and personally I thought it was extremely brave of her to protect herself and stop communication with a person that had clearly brought her so much pain. No one will know what truly happened between the two of them, nor is it any of our business, but to see the public's reaction to someone cutting contact with a parent was a clear indication of how stigmatized it is to set boundaries with family.

Just because someone is family does not mean you have to tolerate abuse. You are allowed to cut family out of your life. If you are unable to cut them out because that would impact your relationship with other family members, then limit the amount of time and access they have to you. Accept that they will not change and stop expecting better from them. In moments where they are suddenly loving, remember their track record of behaviour and do not trust these moments. As much as you will want to, do not leap into those moments to try to build the connection you crave. Recognize that this is momentary, and although they might love you, they do not know how to communicate love.

We often are our worst selves around the people we love because there is an implicit belief that they are stuck with us, won't leave and will put up with us no matter how we treat them. While it is comforting to be safe in the knowledge that your family will be there for you, we need to hold ourselves to a higher standard and not let this expectation allow us to treat relationships that we value with disrespect. Setting boundaries – and understanding that just because someone is family does not mean you are owed a place in their life or that they are owed a place in yours – actually leads to healthier relationships because taking any person for granted will always lead to resentment. The best cure to resentment is boundaries.

Take Action: Writing a family list of boundaries that you all agree to respect is a powerful way to ensure healthy interactions. Sitting down as a family and creating it together is best because, unlike house rules, everyone needs to have a say in boundaries. Give your children a chance to vocalize if they don't feel like they can respect a boundary, so that you can come up with a compromise. For example, let's say one of your children wants the rule to not touch any belongings in someone else's room. The parent then has the opportunity to say, "I agree to that boundary and that means you are now responsible for making your bed every morning and bringing your laundry down to the laundry basket every night." Explaining that they are allowed their boundaries but you are also allowed yours means your whole family can get on the same page.

That's Not Going To Work For Me: Boundaries Around Timekeeping

Thanks to evolving technology, we now have more demands on our time than we could possibly keep up with. If you are saying yes to something, you are in effect saying no to something else, so if your time is spent waiting around for someone, it gets frustrating. Having respect for someone's time is hugely important. As much as it's a cliché that time is our most precious commodity, this becomes true the moment you start to value yourself. When you start believing in your worth, you start to realize that your time is worth something too and it is a privilege for anyone to be in your life. The reason why this is correlated to your self-worth is because when you start to believe you are worth something, the value of your time also increases. It is no longer a shock why people want to spend time with you, and instead of surrounding yourself with those who merely tolerate you, you start taking an active role in choosing people who celebrate you and your existence. Take me for granted and see how quickly I disappear.

When you keep someone waiting, turn up late or cancel at the last minute, what you are telling the person is that you believe your time is more important than theirs. Even if it is done out of carelessness or thoughtlessness, it sends an implicit message that their time is worth wasting. Since we all have a limited amount of time on this earth, no one deserves to have their time wasted – if you want your time to be respected, make sure you are reciprocating that. Take the example of you cancelling plans last minute. The other party might have said no to other plans to spend time with you, and if you had given them more notice, they would have been able to see someone else.

One of the best ways to have good time boundaries is by being honest. We all have a friend who says they are getting on the Tube, when you know they haven't even got in the shower yet. No matter why they do it, whether it's simply habit or out of fear of repercussions, it's disrespectful. I had a friend like this, and how I dealt with it prior to boundaries is I would always tell her to meet me an hour before I was actually going to turn up. Most of the time, we would end up there at the same time. Some of the time, she would be early and would get annoyed that I lecture her about being late and then was late myself and some of the time, she would still be later than the hour. This was not a solution to our problem. The fact is that me communicating that it was disrespectful to keep me waiting for an hour should have been enough, and the fact it wasn't spoke volumes about something I didn't want to acknowledge in our friendship. In fact, when our friendship ended, this was one of the main issues. In our final conversation, I had said she was "unreliable" and she took great offence to that, noting the rare occasions she was on time. What made the years of her perpetual lateness worse was that she would always be dishonest about it. If I could redo that time, I would have had stronger boundaries around this behaviour from the outset. If she was meeting me at mine before heading out and I told her we were leaving at 8 p.m., I would now leave without her if she wasn't there. I remember one time I was waiting at a restaurant for two hours while she did that thing of saying she was on the way, when I could hear the shower on in the background. That wouldn't happen nowadays because I would leave the restaurant after 20 minutes. Back then, I waited for two hours, and in those two hours let that resentment grow and never voiced it upon her arrival. If I had left after 20 minutes, yes, I would probably still be annoyed but I wouldn't have been as annoyed as I was when she turned up two hours late joking that she was worth the wait. It's all about communication, and honesty improves communication.

If you communicate that you are running late, that gives the other party more options. For example, if they haven't left the house yet, they can leave the house later. Being truthful about how late you are running also allows the other party to make a decision about whether to wait for you.

Using an example of a first date, I will wait no longer than 30 minutes as long as you have texted by the time we were meant to be meeting. For example, if we are meeting at 7 p.m. and you are running 20 minutes late, I should have been notified by 7 p.m. that you are running late. Some might think waiting 30 minutes is a long time, and others might think it's not long enough. For me, the calculation comes from the fact that the Tube in London is so unreliable and even with all the planning in the world, once you are stuck, you are often stuck for a while. The importance to me is not the calculation of the time waiting but how it is communicated, as that demonstrates whether this is a person I would want to date.

Looking at two first dates that I happened to have in the same week last year, both guys were late. One texted me saying he would be 30 minutes late, 10 minutes before the date started. I agreed to wait, and upon arrival, he apologized as soon as he arrived. When I offered to get the second round, he declined, saying, "No, don't worry. I was late, let me get this one." He gave warning, he apologized and he made it up to me. Comparing that to the date I went on later that week, he texted me that he would be 10 minutes late, 10 minutes after we were meant to be meeting. After 15 minutes, I texted him, saying, "I am going to wait another 10 minutes but then I'm leaving," and he replied saying he was around the corner. He then turned up 10 minutes after that. There was no apology, he simply said, "Oh great! You got us a table." I waited the same amount of time for both guys but one guy got a second date and the other didn't. I went on three more dates with that first guy and he was never late to another one. It was just bad luck that the first date was the one when he got stuck in traffic but even by his behaviour, it showed it was a rarity and demonstrated respect for my time. Bearing in mind that this is a first date where typically you are on your best behaviour, if you can't even be on time for this, there is no chance that you will be a year into a relationship. In this situation, this was the first time we were meeting, but as a general rule, if you have a track record of being reliable and have good timekeeping skills, that means that on the odd occasion where you have to cancel due to something urgent and unpredicted, people are more forgiving because it isn't a pattern of behaviour.

Much like being late, when people cancel it can be frustrating. Most adults I know have packed lives and if I have given you my time, it's not because I have copious amounts of it, but because I made you a priority. Making time for all the people in your life is a difficult enough task that is made even harder when you don't follow through on those plans. There is a way to cancel with good boundaries, though, and it is largely down to effort. With my job, I often have work opportunities come up at the last minute and so I do cancel a lot. Because I know that, if I make plans that are over a month in advance, I will warn the person that while I'm happy to make plans, there is a chance I will have to cancel. I did this recently when a friend and I both wanted to go see the musical *Hamilton*. The closest tickets we could get were in two months so we chose a date and booked tickets but I warned her that a work thing might come up and that would take priority. She understood and wanted to book it anyway. A month later, a work thing came up, I told her as soon as I knew and she was fine with it because I had already warned her. She didn't mind going with her sister, and I didn't mind losing the cost of the ticket because I had created the inconvenience. We didn't have an issue around it because we communicated.

In instances where it is more last minute, I will always weigh up how important the job opportunity is because it is important you recognize that you are actually making that decision between your career and a friend. The rare occasions the job has won is when it's a longer-term project or when I've had to go abroad unexpectedly so the commitment to the job is greater. In these moments, when I cancel, I always offer an alternative date immediately. I will make all the plans for the next one, and putting that extra effort in makes the difference. If the cancellation was really at the last moment, I will do something special like paying for the meal when we rearrange or sending them flowers to apologize. While I'm not saying you have to do this, I choose to do this because I want my friends to know I value them and their friendship. Even without this added gesture, if it's a rare occurrence, most people are understanding as long as you make the effort to rearrange.

When I have been the person on the receiving end of the cancelling, I also tend to be more forgiving because I know my own job is unpredictable, but also I am more lenient because I believe that it is perfectly acceptable if your career takes priority over the people in your life. I don't believe that is an indication of how much you love and care about them, just an indication that people have different priorities. While the people in my life will always be a higher priority than my job, who am I to judge other people's priorities and decide for them which order their priorities should take? Cancelling on me for your work is not a boundary

I care about personally, as long as the requirements above are met. As long as I'm given enough notice and you are apologetic and make an effort to rearrange, then I'm happy. When I set boundaries is when it is a repeated offence and the disregard of my time is apparent.

I have actually ended a friendship over being cancelled on one too many times. I had not seen this friend in two years after I realized I was the only one to make an effort. The last time we met, she had already cancelled three times and when we finally saw each other, she turned up with her mum without any warning and the only explanation came when her mum went to the loo and she said they were at a workshop and her mum wanted to come and she couldn't say no. I had never met her mum before and considering I had not seen my friend in two years, a large number of things I wanted to talk about were things I would not want to talk about in front of someone I hadn't met. I would rather she had cancelled. After that dinner, she insisted she would make it up to me and we could do dinner just the two of us in the next week. There is a difference in saying you are going to make it up to someone, and actually doing it. The next week turned into the next month and eventually I stopped believing her. In effect, I was distancing from her until I got a call late one evening from New York that her boyfriend was cheating on her. I helped her through that situation and then as soon as it was resolved, she disappeared again, only to resurface another two years later. She wanted to do dinner and I had explained to her that if we made plans, she could not cancel and if she did that would be the last time I would make plans with her. She agreed and we made plans, only for her to message me two days before saying she had confused Monday for Tuesday and asking if we could move our dinner.

> Hey! I got Monday confused with Tuesday. Any chance you can do 2nd instead of 3rd?

I would have had more respect for her if this initial message included an apology and an acknowledgement of the inconvenience she had caused, as well as confronting the boundary I had set.

> Hey! I'm not free on the 2nd and my schedule is pretty packed. I think it's best if we just leave it.

My first message will always say less than more. This low-investment message is the best place to start because my intention was to follow through on the boundary I had set and end the friendship if she cancelled for the fourth time.

> Ohhh I want to see you though. I just made a mistake. How about this, you tell me what works for you?

The language in these texts is interesting because although she is still yet to apologize, the first part states her need, as opposed to acknowledging my feelings or how her change in plan would affect me. The second sentence jumps to defensiveness. In the first two messages alone, there is no accountability for her actions, which confirmed the fact that this is neither a friendship I need or want.

> To be honest, Samantha, this is the fourth time you have moved around dates. It's not really the cancelling as much as the attitude around it, and I'm not sure I'm the same person as when we used to be close.

I have explained my reasoning out of respect for a friendship that was once so close we went travelling together alone for a month. But as the texts go on, I am realizing that this is how our friendship has always worked. The only difference is that I now had the self-esteem to know that my time was just as valuable as hers and I now had the skills to know how to set boundaries.

> Listen, I'm really sorry. I genuinely made a mistake! It feels a little harsh, to be honest. If you tell me when you're free, I'm happy to work around it.

Anytime a person starts a text with "listen", it is aggression. Similar to "I want to see you," it is a prioritization of what they need in that moment, with a disregard for what I have stated in the previous message. Also note that this is actually the first time she apologizes, yet acts as if it's something she has had to say more than once. The accusation of being harsh is textbook and an attempt at trying to gain control in the situation.

> That's fine, that's your right to feel that way.

This is the beginning of me closing the conversation and also a way to demonstrate I am a different person to the person who she used to know who would have caved at the mention of the word "harsh".

> I want to see you.

A reiteration of her needs yet again.

> I understand that you find me harsh and yet I have never given anyone in my life four chances. It has left me with quite a bad taste in my mouth that instead of taking accountability, you are trying to guilt me and shame me and to be honest, that's a shit foundation for a friendship, particularly one that needs rebuilding. Good night x

This last text is optional. I could have just left it at the previous text but my personal preference is to try to conclude the communication whenever possible. I also tend to communicate my reasoning more if I have ever had any respect for the person, even if it was in the past and so seek to give them closure and an understanding, as much as I can. I will attempt to do this once and then leave it. After this text, she continued to keep texting for 10 minutes without a response, another indication of lack of boundaries, and that is when I blocked her number.

As with many situations I have discussed, the conversation that ends the friendship illuminates the problems that were always there to begin with. The response gives you the answer you need. It is rarely the actual issue that ends a friendship but more so, the conversation that follows that highlights the issues that already existed. It had been a problem from the beginning of our friendship that I made more effort than she did and she only got in touch when it was convenient for her. In reality, in those two years, I had changed a lot. She didn't know this new version of me with boundaries so I'm not surprised she didn't take me seriously when I set the boundary initially and said that if we make a plan, she can't cancel. When you change, there will be strong reactions to it because your boundaries will be shocking to them. But as with many examples in this book, the last-minute cancelling was a symptom of a broader issue in our relationship, and setting the boundary just highlighted the lack of respect that was already there in the first place.

Take Action: If you are a constant canceller and always running late, it's time to get yourself some practical solutions. For me, I used to have a physical diary which used to really help to visually see my week laid out. In the last few years, I have swapped to the calendar app on my phone so that it's more accessible. When I have to leave to be somewhere, I will set an alarm on my phone an hour before to get ready and then 10 minutes before I am meant to leave so that I have a warning to finish up and get out of the door. This might seem like the kind of thing you have to do for a child, but if you need tools in order for you to be on time, then use them. It's childish to think you are above using reminders to assist you. It's being an adult to admit your weaknesses and find a practical solution to fix them.

I Don't Have The Emotional Capacity for This Conversation: Boundaries Around Emotional Dumps

There is an expectation in relationships, whether romantic or platonic, that to be a good friend and partner, you are a good listener. You will pick up the phone when they call and when they come home at the end of a bad day, you will sit there and listen to them moan until they are done. What then follows is an unprocessed spiel that they haven't had a moment to sit with or digest themselves. In essence, they have taken their raw emotions and because they are uncomfortable dealing with them or sitting with them, they have handed them over to you. While society has normalized this as an everyday way of conversing, this is an emotional dump. We have all been on the receiving end of one, but we have also been the perpetrators in those situations.

I used to be the worst at emotional dumps. Something would happen and I would want to get rid of the discomfort of a negative emotion so quickly that I wouldn't just text one friend, I would text six. I wouldn't wait for one to reply, it would be a copy-and-paste through my entire contacts list and I would only stop once someone replied and eased my anguish. What's worse than an emotional dump? An emotional dump that you know is going to 10 other people. If it was particularly intense, I would call a friend and even after that conversation was over, I would tend to call another and repeat the same conversation.

The equivalent would be someone taking all the junk they no longer want in their house, filling a bag with it, turning up at your door, and dumping the bag on your doorstep before running away. Now, you have to sort through this bag of crap for them and you are as annoyed as they were with its contents. Emotions work the same way, except the only difference is instead of your house, it is your body and instead of physical objects, it is emotions and energy. In this situation, they are not being a good friend or partner for dropping this bag off at your house. Similarly, you are not doing them a service by taking this bag for them. Doing so means they will never learn how to organize their home, because the next time more crap accumulates, they will just do the same thing. The first time you might let it go, but the second time, you will get more and more annoyed, and resentment will build as you start thinking about how they never even called to give you a warning, or check if you were home first. Instead of letting this build up, a person with boundaries would hand the bag back to them and say, "I love you very much, but you can't just turn up without any notice. I know that it's annoying and potentially uncomfortable to have all this crap in your house, but this is not my crap, it doesn't belong to me and it's not my responsibility. What I can do is support you while you sort through this crap yourself."

At the time of writing this chapter, the world is currently going through the coronavirus pandemic and I am currently on my fourth day of self-isolation. If you remember this time, and I am writing this in the past tense and hoping with every cell in my body that upon publication, this whole ordeal will have ended and life will have returned to normal, you will remember how ever-present the corona conversation was. Everyone was texting about it, every social media post was about it and no matter where you turned it seemed unavoidable. Something that I haven't told people is the reason I am self-isolating is because I currently have the coronavirus. (Congrats to future me on surviving it and actually being able to finish writing your book in the meantime.) I am not telling people because I don't want to contribute to the hysteria and panic in the world, and have specifically not told the 300,000 people who follow me because there is already enough worry. However, as a consequence of my friends and my followers not knowing, I am continuing to get intense and highly emotional messages every single day. It is all a little too much right now and I really need to be prioritizing my self-care, both for my physical health and for my mental health. What better time to teach people how to boundary emotional dumps?

> Hey! Do you have the emotional capacity to talk about coronavirus?

> Hey! To be honest, I'm feeling really overwhelmed at the moment. Are you OK though? Do you have someone else you can talk to?

Swap the word "coronavirus" for anything that is emotionally heavy and can you imagine how much nicer the world would be if we just checked before offloading. The first text allows people to check in with their body and see how they are doing and gives them the opportunity to say no. The reply gives them the chance to be kind and compassionate while also taking care of themselves and not engaging in a conversation that would be to their detriment. If we normalize this kind of etiquette in conversations, the overwhelming feelings many people in the world are currently experiencing don't keep being passed in circles. If the second person wasn't honest, and let the first person offload even if they were not in the headspace to handle it, the likelihood is the second person would then go to another person to vent, and we get stuck in this spiral.

So how do we take care of our own emotions so they don't become the responsibility of others? First of all, we have to realize when we are emotionally dumping.

A trivial example of this from my own life was after speaking at an event with three other influencers. Following the event, I had written an emotional caption for Instagram about a personal memory and about an hour later, I went back on Instagram to see another influencer had copied my caption almost word for word. With any other caption, it probably wouldn't have annoyed me so much but this one had made me cry while writing it. It meant a lot to me and as a result, I felt instant anger. I sent off three texts and my friends replied with all the "OMG HOW ANNOYING" standard replies, and I felt my anger settling down until one of my friends then replied with, "I just commented under her photo." My heart stopped. I didn't want to cause a drama over it. My friend had made a passive-aggressive comment saying, "This caption looks familiar . . ." That is not how I would ever handle that situation. I told her to delete it, and thankfully, the influencer was none the wiser, but because of that outcome, it made me stop and consider what had just happened.

Whenever you get an instant surge of emotion, there is always something larger going on than the incident itself. Yes, someone copying my caption was annoying but it shouldn't have made me *that* angry, which means there was something underneath it. There is a phrase that is often used in Alcoholics Anonymous that says, "If it is hysterical, it is historical." If I had not reacted to my anger but instead sat with it, what I would have realized is that underneath that anger was actually the fact I felt unseen, and because one of my highest values is to be appreciated, I'd reacted more intensely. The personal story I had written in my caption was actually about rejection and so, in writing it, I had already been vulnerable, and when it was copied it felt like my story of rejection had itself been rejected. I believe every situation arises in life to give you an opportunity to heal your past, but instead of using that opportunity to heal what had happened to me, I reacted to the anger. What ensued was another situation that I had to handle that took me away from processing my feelings. My friend, in the most well-meaning way possible, became angry for me. I passed my anger on to her, and she acted on the anger in her body as if it was her own. This is a lack of boundaries on both of our parts. I should have stopped for a moment and felt the anger myself, and she should not have carried my emotions for me. Life can get pretty messy when you don't know whose emotions are whose.

Now I have boundaries in place, I would manage a similar situation by putting my hand on my heart, taking a deep breath and asking myself what I'm feeling. Is it just anger? Is it sadness too? And what does this remind me of from childhood? If I still feel residual anger, I then know that anger is completely about the situation in front of me and not due to past memories, in which case, I would give a little pre-warning to a friend with a simple "I am annoyed. Can I vent to you for a moment?" and then I would talk to them about it. Since we are human, processing it yourself won't happen 100 per cent of the time, but you can *always* ask that question first. To me, it is just politeness, a courtesy, and it gives the other person the opportunity to let you know if something is actually going on in their life which means they can't take on additional emotions.

While I have used a more trivial example above, I also do this in more serious situations. In 2019, I found out a family member had cancer on Christmas Eve and I really needed to talk to someone who was outside of my family. Instead of launching into a very heavy, emotionally intense conversation, I simply texted my friends with a "Hey! Are you busy?" or a "When you are free, can you give me a call?" As I've had my boundaries in place for quite a few years now, my friends know that this is my code for "this is important", but it gives them an opportunity to say that they are busy without being guilted into knowing the severity of the content. There are very few people in the world that upon hearing that your family member has cancer would say they were too busy, which is why I would rather know if the person is busy first. In some cases, people will respond to my text with, "I'm just with people, can I call you in a few hours?" and others will respond with a "Yes, struggling to stay on top of everything right now. Are you OK?", in which case that is my cue to go to someone else.

During this period of my life, I had two or three good friends who had the space in their life to be there for me and check in with me daily. Some friends only had the bandwidth to drop a text once a week to see how I was doing and, for example, one of my best friends had just had a baby so was completely absent in that time of my life. One is not a better friend than another, and the one who could only be there for me in a small way could also be the friend to turn up at my house every day for another event in my life. Similarly, I couldn't be there for my friend in her new parenthood because I was dealing with my own crisis.

Once I learnt how to be boundaried in the way I shared, I found it so much easier to enforce boundaries when others shared with me. As a life coach, I am the person in the friendship group who people tend to consult first. I am the go-to person when everything goes wrong and they need advice. I am also the person they avoid when they want to go back to their ex for the fifteenth time, yet the person whose shoulder they want to cry on when it all goes wrong. And to be honest, having that role as both my job and in my personal life was a lot.

The first thing I took responsibility for was that I was doing my job when I wasn't being asked to. I was giving unsolicited advice when actually a friend wasn't coming to me because I was a life coach, but just coming to me because I would listen, so I introduced a simple sentence: "Do you want me to listen or do you want advice?" Then I would stop feeling the need to respond instantly. As part of my job, I am on my phone a lot because of social media and a lot of my work discussions take place on WhatsApp, but just because I am online, it doesn't mean I am available. In fact, I turned both my read receipts and "last seen" status off. I learnt to say I was busy and then would give them an alternative time that I would be able to speak. It could be something as simple as, "Hey! I'm at work at the moment, can we talk at 6 p.m. tonight?" This sentence completely eradicated any guilt for prioritizing myself and my own mental health. Previously I had taken so much pride in being a "good friend" that I wouldn't look after myself, but recently I found myself in a period of life when I needed my own time and energy more than ever.

I previously have been diagnosed with PTSD from medical trauma and while I have been recovered from it for five years, a recent event in my life suddenly brought up pieces of my past that I had worked with my life coach to heal. It was exhausting, draining and I had very little left to give in the way of time and energy because for the first time in my life, I had the self-esteem to recognize that I needed my sole focus to be on myself. One day a friend asked me for coffee and I apologized and said I didn't have the emotional capacity to be sociable and that I would be in touch at a later date. I was meant to be helping organize a stage show at the time, but was honest and open with the main organizer and said I didn't have the emotional capacity to help. I could still perform but not be involved in the behind-the-scenes setup. I even set boundaries with my closest friends. The closer I am to them, the more honest I will be. Partially because if they are a best friend, we would have already learned how to communicate boundaries over and over, but also because I am able to be more casual in the way I phrase it. One day when my best friend was moaning about the same relationship problem she refuses to do anything about, I responded with, "I don't have the emotional capacity for this." She dropped it and we moved on. Among friends who aren't used to boundaries, this might seem cruel, but when boundaries become part of the norm of your friendship, something like this is actually a non-event.

A few weeks later, a tweet went viral about setting boundaries. The controversy around it was due to the fact the person had phrased their boundaries in a very formal way. My best friend and I were talking about it, so I brought up the fact that the way I set boundaries with her is very casual and she said she preferred the way I communicated it because it was more human and it was the way I speak normally. She also said that it was appropriate given the context and that if her mum died, I would not have just said, "I don't have the emotional capacity for this." She's right; I most certainly would not have. A lot of the time when this conversation of boundaries and emotional capacity arises online, the comments are filled with examples like this. They will take an extreme example like your dad dying in a car crash and make witty retorts like, "So if someone dies, you are going to tell them to get back to you in five to seven working days," as an attempt to invalidate the message of boundaries and suggest it is coldhearted, forgetting the fact that it is necessary that you use common sense when you decide to set boundaries. Boundaries are your choice and so you only set them if you decide if they are appropriate. Those erroneous Twitter comments always remind me of a situation that I heard about. A friend's mother had died in a sudden and really traumatic way and my friend had invited three of her closest friends to not only attend the funeral but help support her through it. One of the friends found funerals really difficult, but out of obligation felt like she couldn't say no to her friend so she went. In order to cope, she ended up getting really drunk and chain-smoked to survive it. She even smoked in the service, while making loud remarks about how morbid everything was and how uncomfortable she was. She got so drunk that one of the friends had to take her home, and as a result, instead of having three friends there to lean on, the grieving friend only had one. Of course, it would be simple to say that she should not have gotten drunk, or smoked or made loud remarks but all of that could have been avoided if she had just been able to say she didn't have the emotional capacity to be her support system. I'm sure everyone, including her grieving friend, would have much preferred that to what happened instead. So when people want to use extreme examples involving death, this is the story I tell them. Your limits are your limits and if you can be honest with yourself about how much you can handle, that is better than feeling obligated to do something and then adding more to that hurting person's plate. It would have been kinder to say no.

The point is not to become a cold person who doesn't do or care about anything that doesn't serve themselves.

The purpose is to create choice and freedom. When you are free to choose, you realize that a lot of the time you actively choose to help the people in your life – but only when you are actually able to help and not when it comes at the expense of yourself.

Take Action: When dealing with emotionally heavy subjects, the conversations can escalate really quickly if you aren't careful. There is a lot of stigma nowadays about how women use too many softeners in their language. While that is a valid conversation, if you use them consciously, they can be really powerful. My friends and I are now so honest that occasionally my friends will say, when asked if they want honesty, "No, I'm too sensitive right now," and we move on. Adding these softeners, as well as others, including "I was wondering . . ." or "Perhaps you could . . ." are really helpful. If making my boundaries gentler results in less defensiveness, then that's an intentional choice I make. This is because communicating boundaries in a written context, whether that's a text or an email, can be interpreted differently or heard with a different tone of voice than intended. Alternatively, if I want to keep a boundary short and I don't want that shortness to come across as harshness, I will just add an emoji to almost communicate "I'm not angry." As silly as it sounds, "That doesn't work for me" and "That doesn't work for me <3" get interpreted very differently.

Text Templates

Most of the time when people ask me how to phrase boundaries, they aren't really asking me for the words, but for how to say it. Usually, they want to know how to say it politely and in this instance, the obsession with politeness is still an attempt to control the response. No matter how polite you are, the person on the receiving end of your boundary setting might still react badly.

In most of these examples below, I keep it simple. I write out exactly what I want to say because that's the best way to set boundaries, by speaking from the heart. It's saying what you mean and meaning what you say, nothing less and nothing more. Giving out text templates is always difficult without context or the full situation but I felt it was important to include some in this book so that you have an example of the language that you can use. I also hope this proves that boundaries can be set in a kind and compassionate way. I have a particularly direct way of speaking (I think it comes from my Chinese side), so as I previously mentioned, how I personally communicate that this is not coming from an angry place is to add emojis, even just a heart at the end makes it come across less harsh. When using these text templates, please personalize them – that is important. When you tell someone how much you love them, include examples to lighten the mood. When you tell someone how they come across as insensitive, use their previous wording. These are nuances I would not be able to add into this chapter but they are essential for your own boundary conversations.

Situation: *My partner dumps her mental illness on me. How do I kindly tell her that it's getting too much?*

Template:

"Hey love, can I talk to you about something? I know you are going through a lot with your mental health and I want to support you, but I have reached the stage where I need to also take care of myself in order for our relationship to be the healthiest it could possibly be. I love you very much and I think it's important for both of us that I'm not the only person you rely on when you want to talk about your mental health. It would really help if you asked me about me first or just checked in with me, the way I just checked in with you before offloading. It would help me feel like the support is mutual in our relationship and it would also give me a chance to mentally prepare."

Situation: *My girlfriend and my mum don't get on. They frequently come to me to talk about their issues and they insult each other. It is really hurtful.*

Template:
To your girlfriend:

> "I understand that what my mum says is upsetting, but I am going to need you to learn how to communicate with her directly. It is not my responsibility to fix your relationship and I will be telling her the same thing. In the meantime, I expect you to speak about my mum with respect as I would not tolerate her talking about you in a disrespectful way as well."

To your mum:

> "I understand that you do not like my girlfriend, but I need you to respect the fact I have chosen this woman as my partner. I understand that you do not agree, but that does not allow you to treat her with disrespect. I would not allow her to talk about you in a disrespectful manner so I would appreciate it if that is reciprocated."

Situation: *I think my friend is angry at me because they are not responding to my texts. What do I say?*

Template:

> "Hey! I have noticed your lack of response and I'm wondering if you are OK. If there is an issue between us, I would love if you could communicate that so we can work through it. Miss you xx"

Situation: *I slept with a guy and ever since he has been replying slower and with shorter replies, and it's making me feel bad. How do I tell him that it isn't OK?*

Template:

> "Hey! I've felt that you've been more distant since we slept together. If that is the case, I would much rather you communicated that and just let me know that you are not interested. This is starting to make me feel a bit shit and I'd appreciate the honesty xx"

Situation: *A friend keeps using my friend's death to emotionally manipulate me. How do I end the friendship?*

Template:

> "Hey! I really didn't like that you used my friend's death against me. I told you that in confidence and it has broken my trust that you used that private information to hurt me. It felt manipulative [or however you felt] and I don't feel comfortable being friends with someone who behaves like that. Take care xx"

Situation: *My friends bring up my trauma randomly and I find it triggering. How do I tell them to stop?*

Template:

> "That time in my life was really difficult for me and when you bring it up without warning, it takes me off guard and reminds me of a time in my life I would rather forget. I would really appreciate it if you could respect my wishes and not bring it up in the future."

Situation: *My boss will ask me to do work, give me a deadline and then a week before the deadline is due will ask me where the piece of work is and it makes me feel like I'm going crazy and bad at my job. How do I tell her to stop?*

Template:

> "Hey! I have noticed that you tend to give me deadlines and then ask for the work before it is due. I have never submitted work late and it would be great if you could trust me with the deadlines you give. If you would like to make the deadlines tighter to give yourself more time to review it, that's totally fine, but I would prefer it if you could give me a deadline we both can stick to. It would really help me prioritize my workload to be able to organize my tasks in urgency and I would really appreciate it."

Situation: *My boss raises his voice a lot. How do I ask him to stop?*

Template:

> "Please do not speak to me like that. I do not think it is appropriate in a place of work to be shouting."

Situation: *My friend is always talking about the plastic surgery they want and it makes me feel bad about my appearance. Am I allowed to ask them to stop or am I being selfish?*

Template: If a conversation is making you feel bad, then you don't need to partake in it. It doesn't make you wrong or them wrong, but it is within your right to ask to change the conversation. Here are some ways to change the topic:

- "Can we talk about something else?"
- "Do you have someone else you can talk to about plastic surgery?"
- "Plastic-surgery conversations don't make me feel good about myself. Let's change the conversation."

Situation: *A friend never listens to me and when I share a story, she always tops it with a better one and I find it frustrating. I don't want to end the friendship without trying to address it first, but how do I phrase it?*

Template:

> "For this friendship to work, I'm going to need you to listen to me when I talk. I find it hard to share things with you when you revert the conversation back to yourself when I'm not finished."

Situation: *My boyfriend always moans about using a condom and I'm so bored of fighting about it. How do I be firm about it so he won't keep bringing it up?*

Template:

"We have had this conversation before. I am not having sex without a condom. No matter how many times you bring it up, I will not be changing my mind and I don't want to repeat this conversation again. I shouldn't be guilted for caring about both of our protection and it really ruins the mood whenever this conversation comes up. If you want to have sex, then a condom is needed."

Situation: *A former toxic friend has moved back into town and is now going to the same university as me and wants to be friends again. How do I tell her I don't want to be friends?*

Template:

"Hey! I'm in a really different place from when you left town. I'm not the same person as when you left and I don't know that a friendship would be healthy for us at the moment. I hope you are enjoying your time at [enter university name] though xx"

Situation: *One of my friends just told me he likes me more than a friend. How do I turn him down without it affecting the friendship?*

Template: Your reply can't guarantee the friendship won't be affected because it depends on his feelings as well but as long as your reply is kind and compassionate, it gives you a better chance. Try something like this:

"Hey! Thank you for telling me that, I really appreciate your honesty. I value you as a friend and I'd like to keep our relationship that way as I don't see us as anything more. You mean a lot to me and I know how much courage it took to share that with me and thank you for letting me know. Xx"

Situation: *My sister keeps taking pictures and videos of me without my permission and then posting them, joking about how ugly I look. It makes me really upset, how do I tell her to stop?*

Template:

"It is not OK that you keep taking pictures of me. I do not find your jokes funny and it is really hurtful. I am asking you to stop and I need you to listen to my request."

Situation: *My partner makes more money than me and when she chooses a restaurant, it is normally out of my price range and it is creating a lot of financial pressure on me. How do I change this?*

Template:

> "I would love to go out for dinner. Can we choose another place though? It is out of my price range and I want to be able to enjoy my time with you without worrying about money xx"

Situation: *My boss likes to micromanage me and constantly interrupts me for updates. It makes it hard to focus and as a result, to appease his nagging, I submit work before I feel it is ready. How do I ask him to stop?*

Template:

> "I know you really care about the work we are doing and I want to reassure you that I do as well. I have been finding it difficult to be as efficient as I would like to be as I find the updates distracting. Would it be possible to update you as soon as I have completed the work? That way I can ensure I have a chance to proofread my own work before you review it?"

Situation: *My stepdad smokes around our children and I worry about the second-hand smoke. When I tell him to go outside, he doesn't listen. How do I insist?*

Template:

"I have told you that it isn't OK when you smoke inside the house. If you won't go outside to smoke, then you won't be allowed in my house again. I will do whatever is necessary to protect my children and I am asking that you respect the rules in my house."

SETTING BOUNDARIES IN DIFFERENT CONTEXTS

CHAPTER 5:

YOUR NEW LIFE

Now that you have all the tools in order to make changes in your life, now is the time to start implementing them and before you know it, you will start to see your life change. At first, people become uncomfortable around the changes in you that they are seeing, but over time as you find your new balance and boundaries become a part of your norm, you will start to see why this is all worth it. Since giving out this advice online, I've been able to see first-hand how boundaries have such a positive impact from messages I receive daily. The most common thing I hear is how simple their life is now and how liberating it is to say how they feel. I get stories from people who set boundaries around emotional dumping with their partner and write to me to tell me how much healthier their relationship has become with just one conversation and how they wonder why they didn't do it sooner. I get messages saying how they set a boundary with a friend for the first time and it went better than they could have imagined. People tell me about times when they have finally raised their voice about an issue that has been ongoing and being firm and clear made them feel so confident.

With each message, I'm even more convinced of the power of boundaries.

It's hard to describe or quantify how my life has changed since I incorporated boundaries, but it's safe to say they have invaded every area of my life. I am not only better at setting them, but I am also far better at respecting them. They go hand in hand. When someone sets a boundary with me, there is a small part of me that oozes with pride for them, even if the consequence is inconvenient for me, because someone looking after themselves and standing up for themselves is a beautiful thing.

In my love life, the way I am treated is incomparable to before. There is a point in everyone's journeys that you will look back at your old life and won't recognize your past self as the same person. The moment this happened in my love life was when I was ending it with a guy I had been on five dates with. I was so used to the fact that rejecting men inevitably ends in words that hurt that I knew the quality of people I was dating shifted when not only did he accept the end of our relationship with grace but also complimented me in the final text and thanked me for my honesty. Long gone are the days of being "too nice".

In my friendship groups, the friends I keep are so special. In the middle of my "mass exodus", I remember convincing myself that it was impossible to find new friendships in adulthood. I told myself people didn't have the time and even if they did, that time would go to old friends, not new ones. How wrong I was. I am so glad I went through the heartbreak of losing my old friends to find people who truly cared. About a year after my mass exodus, my dad got diagnosed with cancer and I entered one of the hardest times in my life. It was my new friends that held me together through it all. I wouldn't have been able to say the same about the people I used to call friends.

Boundaries are the reason I lost all my old friends but they're also the reason why I gained better ones in their place. I have people in my life who respect me, and as someone who chased being liked for so long, I wouldn't have believed that respect would feel so much better than being liked. To have the respect of the people you yourself respect and being able to call those people loved ones is special. My friendships now are so simple. Eliminating bitching and gossiping in my friendship groups has made group dynamics easy – there is a natural ease and trust among my friends that I wish I had had when I was younger. I now have the friends I always deserved and I only have people in my life I can trust. In fact, my friends are my daily reminders of how incredible humans can be and yes, that doesn't always take away the pain of a lost friendship, but if I had to do it all over again, I would, because it was all worth it for the quality of people I have in my life now. If your friends truly are a reflection of who you are, then I would happily have any friend of mine be a reflection of me and me of them and that's not a sentence I could have said a few years ago.

In terms of my career, the greatest reminder of how much I have changed is the fact that I receive messages daily calling me The Queen Of Boundaries. It's a compliment, an honour and frankly, a shock to the inner child in me. For someone who struggled so much in the beginning with how to articulate the simplest of boundaries, I never would have thought this is where I would end up. I would be remiss if I pretended that boundaries have only brought me positivity. I am way more disliked than I was before boundaries and I hate that this is part of the journey, but it is, and it's not an option. I have had moments where I have struggled with it and what has helped me move past it is the realization that my difficulty with it is simply because I'm not used to it. My life's purpose for a long time was to be liked by everyone, but that didn't work out very well. I lost myself, I didn't know who I was and the parts I did know, I didn't like. I was liked by everyone but I disliked myself. I much prefer my way of life now. It might bring me more hate than before (especially online!), but life is a lot more fun when you like yourself. There is a certain kind of liberation when you are disliked for being yourself and you choose to continue to be you anyway. My love for myself is not worth the cost of other people's approval. And if you think for a moment it is, then the cost is not only boundaries but also confidence – people tend to hate confident women more than they hate insecure ones. When you are confident, outspoken, ask for what you need and have the audacity to set boundaries, you become a symbol of something that other people believe they can't have. Jealousy and envy come in, not because boundaries are not accessible to everyone, but because it takes a certain bravery to believe you deserve them.

One day you wake up, you realize you've changed and you won't believe how strong your boundaries are. Or maybe it's a matter of mini-moments and small realizations of gradual growth. For me, one of the moments I remember was an evening when a friend was trying to convince me to go to a house party that I didn't want to go to. She asked me once, I said no, she asked me twice, I told her I had already said no and she asked me a third time and I simply responded with "boundaries", and the conversation was over. We both ended up laughing and I couldn't help but smile at the fact that I spent so long learning how to articulate boundaries and now I rarely need to, because the mere mention of the word "boundaries" gets the conversation dropped. In these moments, I barely recognize the old me and yet I am so proud of that younger version of myself, the one who made all the mistakes and meant so well but hurt so much as a result. That person with no boundaries made me into who I am today. Without her, there would be no me, but anyone who confuses me for her now gets met with boundaries.

When you start this journey, it is hard to imagine what a life with strong boundaries will look like. Although there is no way to give you a full picture until you live it yourself, as I am writing this final chapter, I am currently on holiday with a friend and it's occurred to me that the best examples of boundaries are in the small and subtle moments. One was a moment when we had decided to go paddleboarding and when we both arrived on the beach, I changed my mind because it was too cold. I said so and my friend replied, "Yeah, it's a bit cold, isn't it?" She didn't want to go either, but it got me thinking – what if I hadn't said what I was thinking? Would we both have ended up paddleboarding to please the other, while neither of us actually wanted to do it? It sounds stupid, but this happens all the time. It's in the little moments. My friend has just gone to explore the other end of the beach; I didn't want to go so she went alone.

Boundaries mean we are separate humans. I don't worry that I'm disappointing her and she doesn't need my company to enjoy herself. I just came back from getting lunch, she wasn't hungry so I went by myself. A life without boundaries would have meant I would have been hungry in silence simply to not be difficult or because shame would have told me that my needs were unimportant and that I should be ashamed that my hunger is greater than my friend's. Another example is when my friend wanted to go on a hike the other day. At the moment, I am still recovering from having previously had coronavirus and it has knocked my fitness right out of me, which means we walk at completely different paces. I agreed to go, but under the condition that we go at my pace and that she would not complain, moan or sigh in any way. This was not an implication that she would do any of these things but more a setting of boundaries before they were needed. I no longer wait for the line to be crossed to set boundaries.

Similarly, the night before, I had fallen asleep in the middle of an episode of *Fleabag* and the following night I wanted to rewatch the episode before we moved on to a new one. My friend agreed as long as I agreed to then stay awake for two more episodes. Both situations were such small discussions that most people wouldn't even describe them as boundary setting, but without both of us asking for what we needed, each situation could have easily caused passive-aggressive comments or resentment. A small thing like me falling asleep again, and her feeling like she had wasted her time, could easily lead to annoyance that would fester in another part of our trip. Instead, we communicated and she took responsibility for her own needs being met and I took responsibility for mine. It's in these moments that the differences are glaring not because it's a big moment but because it makes me aware of how many situations could be avoided by simply asking a few more questions or speaking up.

Being five years into this journey, it's not that my boundaries are never broken, it's that it takes me less time to notice. I never justify myself anymore and I have the confidence to set boundaries in a way I never did before. Every time I build stronger boundaries, my threshold for bullshit gets lower and my tolerance for disrespect goes down. Of course, I still slip up occasionally. Sometimes I let a person get away with too much or I hesitate to say something in the moment. That is human. It is easy to fall into your old patterns when those behaviours were so ingrained in you for so long. Thankfully, boundaries don't have a time limit. That means as long as I'm forgiving towards myself, I can fix it as soon as I notice it. Remind yourself that at the root of boundaries is self-love and therefore it serves no purpose if the tool that is designed to protect you is being used to harm you. Over time, you begin to trust yourself because you know that you have the communication skills to navigate any difficult conversations.

Be kind to your younger version of yourself who didn't know what you know now. Your lack of boundaries served a purpose at one point in your life. Taking care of others first and foremost was something you learned in order to protect yourself, and those habits and behaviours might take a while to unlearn. Be gentle with yourself and allow yourself to make mistakes, forgive yourself for it and learn from it.

You are about to begin this exciting new journey. Look forward to the new you that you are about to meet. That new you will ruffle some feathers, but embrace it. Every time anyone is disgruntled that your boundaries create inconvenience for them, know that you are on the right path. And if anyone calls you selfish, you can now agree with them. After all, there's nothing like the joy of being selfish!

ACKNOWLEDGEMENTS

When I think about how this book came together, I get emotional thinking about how everything aligned so perfectly, not only with the timing but the people who entered my life just when I needed them.

Thank you so much to Michelle Zelli, the person who taught me everything I know about boundaries. Thank you for modelling what an empowered woman looks like, being patient when I fought you every step of the way and most of all for holding space for me in a way that no one else ever has.

Thank you so much to my incredible literary agent, Hayley. I can't convey to you how much it means to me that you never lost hope in the fact I would create another book one day. Thank you for getting excited with every silly idea that didn't pan out and telling me that I'm a good writer on days that I couldn't convince myself. What I love most though is that our journeys of learning and enforcing boundaries coincided and it's been amazing watching us both find our voices, even more so than before!

Thank you so much to Issy and the entire team at Welbeck. This whole process has been such a joy and

ACKNOWLEDGEMENTS

I couldn't be more grateful that you have given me the opportunity to write a book on this topic. From the moment we met, you all were so on board with the message I wanted to send and it means the world to have felt so instantly understood.

To my wonderful social agent, Jamie, I was so close to quitting if it wasn't for you. Thank you for always believing in me more than I believe in myself and for championing me more times than I am even aware of. Thank you for allowing me to be human, in an industry that rarely allows it, and always being there for me – I appreciate it more than I can say.

To my friends and family, thank you for sticking with me through the messy conversations and bumpy road of building the new me. It hasn't always been easy but for those of you who have survived the transition, you are truly the best of the best. To those who didn't, I am grateful for everything that you taught me and thank you for loving me at a time when I didn't love myself.

And to all my followers and readers, thank you for being with me throughout this evolution. There is something so beautiful about having space on the internet where you are accepted for truly being yourself. Being my authentic self comes so naturally to me now because of the safe space that you all provided online, loving me in all my different quirks and weirdness. I hope seeing my passion for boundaries grow in real-time provided you with the proof and evidence that you can do it too.

THE JOY OF BEING SELFISH